America's Famous and Historic Trees

America's Famous

From George Washington's Tulip Poplar

AND HISTORIC TREES

TO ELVIS PRESLEY'S PIN OAK

JEFFREY G. MEYER

with Sharon Linnéa

A FRANCES TENENBAUM BOOK

Houghton Mifflin Company

Boston   New York   2001

For information about permission to reproduce selections from
this book, write to Permissions, Houghton Mifflin Company,
215 Park Avenue South, New York, New York 10003.

Visit our Web site: www.houghtonmifflinbooks.com.

Library of Congress Cataloging-in-Publication Data

Meyer, Jeffrey G.
    America's famous and historic trees : from George Washington's tulip
poplar to Elvis Presley's pin oak / Jeffrey G. Meyer ; with Sharon Linnéa.
      p. cm.
    "A Frances Tenenbaum book."
    ISBN 0-618-06891-0
    1. Historic trees — United States.   2. Historic sites — United States.
    3. United States — History, Local.   I. Linnéa, Sharon.   II. Title.
    E159 .M53   2001
    973 — dc21   00-068245

A Lark Production

Book design by Anne Chalmers
Typeface: Hoeffler Text

Printed in the United States of America
DOW 10 9 8 7 6 5 4 3 2 1

For my wife, Anne;

our sons, Forest and Scott;

and our two Chesapeakes, Tia and Ginny,

who have all given me the inspiration and support

for my life as a tree planter, and who share

my love of the outdoors and

wild places.

Perhaps the oldest living thing east of the Mississippi River, the Angel Live Oak is believed to be nearly 1,400 years old. The tree grows on Johns Island near Charleston, South Carolina.

❧ CONTENTS

 ACKNOWLEDGMENTS

Heartfelt thanks to Susan Corbett for filling in the blanks; to Florence Swanstrom for the great research support; to Michelle Robbins for paying attention to the details; to Frances Tenenbaum for her enthusiasm and encouragement; to Dan O'Connell for getting the message out there; to Karen Watts for wrapping it all up; to Gary Hoover for his artistic support; to Mike Venema for making this possible; to Scot Miller for great photography at Walden Woods; to Charlie Skinner for taking the time to talk with me; to Deborah Gangloff, Rick Crouse, and everyone else at American Forests who has shared the vision of the Famous & Historic Trees project.

America's Famous and Historic Trees

 INTRODUCTION

My Magnificent Obsession

Jeff Meyer beside the linden he planted when he was five years old.

THE AUTUMN I WAS twelve years old, my uncle Buddy and I did a mysterious thing. We went out into the back yard, where there were four magnificent walnut trees that my great-uncle Bill, Buddy's dad, had planted many years before. We traversed the entire yard, picking up five or six hundred large walnut seeds and stuffing them into gunnysacks. Then we hauled them down into the dark basement and left them there.

I probably would have thought this was odd if I didn't idolize my uncle Buddy. He was a scoutmaster who loved the outdoors. At least once a winter, he saw to it that he and I went out in the forest after a deep snowfall, cleared a site, built a small fire, and cooked a full hot dinner that we consumed there in the frigid air. He no doubt thought it gave me character, and you know, I think it did.

Well, the next spring, Uncle Buddy and I headed back downstairs for our walnut stash. We loaded them into his pickup truck and headed four miles north to Homestead, Iowa. We spent the day planting all five hundred of those seeds up and down the banks of the Iowa River. We didn't own the land, we were simply being neighborly, doing a good deed—planting a shadier future for whoever wanted to enjoy it.

That night when I tumbled into bed, exhausted, muscles aching, I think I was about as happy as I'd ever been.

(right) Anne Meyer and young Forest beside the Jacksonville Treaty Live Oak.

(below) Forest with the fifteen-year-old live oak grown from the acorn he picked up when he was a toddler.

My grandmother, Oma, also played a great part in fostering my love of the outdoors and of growing things. She lived next door to us in Amana, Iowa. She was a gardener and she took it *seriously.* Oma had terraced the hill behind her house, and she grew all sorts of wonderful flowers and vegetables there. I was expected to help in the garden, and she was patient as I planted the seeds that seemed interesting to me: strawberries or pole beans, which the ad claimed would grow ten feet tall. As I got older, I had a brainstorm. I got Oma to give me one terrace on which to plant my own garden—but instead of vegetables I planted white pines and other trees. I admit, it wasn't so much about loving trees at that point—it was about laziness. No more daily weeding for me! Plant the trees, water them, and check back in a few years! But I did realize during that time that I loved the outdoors and somehow wanted to incorporate it into my life's work.

I thought about that a lot during the winter of 1980, as I traveled the roads of Florida. I had graduated from Vanderbilt University the year before, married my sweetheart, Anne, and moved to Anne's native Southlands. My major in college had been history and business administration—now there's a practical combination, I'd often thought to myself, Who's in the business of history? But my goal was to have my own business one day. Doing what, I wasn't certain.

My first job out of college was in sales. But as much as I admired the company I worked for and its products, I was restless. I chafed at having an office and a desk, and I hated the jacket and tie. The job required me to make sales calls all over central Florida. As I crisscrossed the state, I was amazed to see how much construction was going on—new housing developments and many strip malls. The thing that saddened me most was seeing magnificent mature trees uprooted and dying to make way for asphalt.

Then one day I read an article about a newly developed machine called a tree hoe that was designed especially for digging up large trees with their roots intact so that they could be moved and replanted. That very day I talked to Anne, then called my dad and Uncle Buddy. They agreed that this sounded like the perfect career opportunity for me. Uncle Buddy, who was a professional trucker, went to Arkansas to pick up the tree hoe. (I was about to go into business with a tree hoe, but I had no idea how to drive one!)

Jubilant, I was out of sales the next day. Finally my heart was dictating how my energies were being spent.

Now I was talking to builders and developers, telling them how greatly their properties would benefit if, instead of bulldozing all their trees, they hired my new company to dig them up and move them to a new location. As it turned out, the developers didn't need much convincing. It was an idea whose time had come.

As Anne and I started our own nursery and orchard, we also started our family. Our first son arrived in 1983, and aptly enough, we named him Foerstner after my grandfather—Forest for short.

Our home was in Jacksonville, and one of our favorite activities was to picnic in the blocks of shade provided by the incredible Treaty Oak that presided over downtown Jacksonville. I was fasci-

Seedlings from a historic tree growing in a planting tray.

Massachusetts children celebrate the tree they planted on the Johnny Appleseed Trail tour.

nated by the plaque that said Chief Osceola had used the area as a campground and had held war councils there; legend has it that many treaties were signed under the tree.

One day when Forest was less than a year old, he toddled back over to our picnic blanket, an acorn clutched tightly in his little hand. Seized by inspiration, we took it home and planted it in our front yard.

Not long thereafter, I was reading a publication of American Forests, the nation's oldest conservation organization, which I'd belonged to for years. The article described how the Japanese emperor had brought the first of Washington's famous Tidal Basin cherry trees as a gift to President Taft and the American people in 1912. (Actually, the first trees had died because they'd been kept in quarantine too long, but Japan kindly sent replacements.) In 1986 American Forests was taking cuttings from those trees to grow their descendants.

Somehow, that fact resonated with what Anne and I had just done in planting an acorn from the Treaty Oak. I knew that American Forests had listings of more than two hundred famous and historic trees throughout the United States. What if we could gather seeds from them and let people plant descendants of trees that had graced the homes of George Washington, Frederick Douglass, or Amelia Earhart? The more I thought about the idea, the more excited I became. I guess it was the history buff finally colliding with the tree man.

I met with some people at American Forests to explain my

passion and my dream. Fortunately, they shared my enthusiasm, and I became the nurseryman for the Famous & Historic Trees project. What a great project it has become! We wrote to communities and historic sites and began to gather seeds and grow them into saplings. At the same time I visited schools, telling kids why it is so important to grow trees. After about ten schools, I knew I was doing an important thing. And the dream was nurtured.

Since 1987 I have grown trees that have been planted in all fifty American states. I've spoken to innumerable schools, Rotary Clubs, and garden clubs, appeared on radio and television programs, even done a special for PBS. I've planted trees at the White House, the Russian White House, and the palace at Versailles in France. And do you know what? My dream, like the trees, has only grown.

Trees are an international symbol of peace. I believe in my heart that most people on earth are good and that every country on earth has its own unique history and stories to tell. My mission is to help each country select a tree that has stood as witness to its people and its history, to preserve that tree and tell its story, to promote understanding among all peoples. A lofty goal, I know, but I believe it can be done.

Meanwhile, I love my job. I can't think of anything more rewarding. Without exception, I've found that helping someone plant a tree is a positive experience, and people who plant trees are positive, forward-looking people.

I once got an anguished call from an elderly lady who lived some thirty miles from Jacksonville. She still lived in the house she'd grown up in, but to say the neighborhood had changed was an understatement. In fact, hers was the only private home left in what had become a bustling commercial area. All of her neighbors' homes were long gone, and she was surrounded by businesses and stores. And yet she'd kept up her lovely and homey house. Unfortunately, a giant storm had ripped through the county and had killed five or six beautiful trees in her yard. When I came to her home, she showed me what had happened, and we mourned those fine old trees together.

What would she do? Almost anyone else might have finally sold the property for the huge amount of money it was now worth to developers. But not my friend. She wanted to replant. And so we did, planting thirty large oak trees that would live for a hundred years after she was gone. I had to love her hope for the future.

I've also helped the Congressional Medal of Honor Society start a project to plant a tree to honor each of the more than 3,400 Congressional Medal of Honor recipients. What a great privilege it has been to meet these people, and what wonderful stories they have! Here in Jacksonville, I've helped organize the planting of more than 5,000 trees. After twenty years, our total is over 100,000. You might say it's become an obsession.

Last weekend I was driving down U.S. 27, south of Orlando. And there I saw a new development of nice houses, without one single tree. I fervently hope that some magnanimous souls will invest in this new neighborhood the way Uncle Buddy used to—by planting trees. I can't think of any investment that pays such great dividends so quickly and lasts for so long.

Forest now has a brother named Scott. The year after he was born, we planted a crape myrtle in the back yard for him. And Forest's oak tree? The fifteen-year-old tree has now flourished to forty feet tall. I hope that for decades to come, Forest and Scott will drive past "their" trees the same way I visit "my" trees in Iowa.

And I hope that after you read this book, you will do the same with the trees you'll be inspired to plant.

1

INDIAN MARKER PECAN

I was born upon the prairie, where the wind blew free and there was nothing to break the light of the sun. I was born where there were no enclosures and where everything drew a free breath. I want to die there and not within walls. I know every stream and every wood between the Rio Grande and the Arkansas. I have hunted and lived all over that country. I lived like my fathers before me, and like them, I lived happily.

—Parra Wa-Samen (Ten Bears), a Yamparika Comanche, in *Bury My Heart at Wounded Knee*

WHEN YOU LOOK at the cities and suburbs of the modern American plains and the Southwest, it's sometimes hard to imagine what life was like there only two hundred years ago. These plains were Comanche territory (whose name means "enemy" in Ute). The Comanche were warriors and wanderers; the tribe was made up of as many as thirty-eight bands that were related only by loose friendship.

They were the most skillful horseback riders and the fiercest warriors and became known to American settlers as "the lords of the plains." The most elite bands of Comanche warriors, called Lobos, or "wolves," were distinguished by their decorative clothing and jewelry, including wolf belts that reached to the ground. The Lobos never retreated in battle, no matter how badly outnumbered they were. Even if the chief commanded the other braves to retreat, the Lobos had to hold their ground to the end. (In fact, if any Lobos withdrew from battle, the families of those who were killed would hunt them down and kill them.) Bravery and hunting and fighting skills were most highly prized. The Lobos were also favored by the women of the tribe, though you might wonder why—a relationship with a Lobo would not seem to be guaranteed longevity.

Although white settlers lived in terror of these warriors, and some of their practices might seem savage to us, the Comanche tribe had very strict rules of honor and conduct. One story was that of nine-year-old Cynthia Ann Parker, the daughter of white settlers, who was taken captive by the Comanche. Cynthia showed great courage and bravery and was adopted into the tribe. She grew up to marry a chief of the Antelope band named Peta Nocona. They had two children, Quanah Parker, a boy, and Prairie

COMMON NAME: Pecan

SCIENTIFIC NAME: *Carya illinoensis*

AKA: pecan hickory, sweet pecan, Illinois nut, soft-shelled hickory

STATE TREE: Texas

Indian tribes frequently tied a small tree to the ground to mark a good camping site.

Flower, a girl. In 1860, when her husband's band was defeated by Texas Rangers, the Rangers were shocked to find a Comanche woman with blue eyes, and they eventually returned Cynthia and Prairie Flower to the Parker family. Cynthia was miserable not knowing the fate of her husband or son. When little Prairie Flower died of an illness, Cynthia died soon thereafter, it is said, of a broken heart. Quanah became the last great chief of the Comanche and the last holdout among the Indian nations against life on a reservation.

For centuries before that, as Ten Bears said, these migrating bands came to know their territory well. Before the arrival of the Spanish settlers, travel was hard, as horses were few and dogs did much of the hauling. But by the mid-eighteenth century, the Comanche had significantly enlarged their herds of horses and become more mobile.

Roving bands of Comanche warriors needed well-marked campsites, and that's what the loosely affiliated bands did for each other. A good Comanche campsite had to be near running water (as a source of fish as well as water), and it had to have tall bluffs or hills on at least three sides for lookouts. Very often the campsite also had a pecan grove. For the Comanche, a pecan grove usually signaled good soil for other fruits and berries and abundant wildlife for hunting. The pecans were also used widely for food and dye.

As you can imagine, there were no Fodor's Guides back then to mark a four-star campsite. But the Comanche, whose lifestyles were of necessity in tune with nature, had natural ways of sending each other messages. When they found a great campsite in which to set up their tipis, they would take a young pecan tree, usually three to five feet tall, and bend it, staking the top to the ground. The tree would thus become a "marker" tree, growing horizontally along the ground before continuing to grow vertically. The campground would be marked for generations to come.

The Comanche, as well as other tribes, used trees for a variety of purposes. There were "turnaround trees," which marked the boundaries of hunting territories; "sacred trees," which were used in the sun dance and could become places of worship; "butchering trees," from which buffalo were suspended and stripped; "annuity trees," under which payments were received, and, of course, "marker trees," which not only denoted campsites but marked trails and meeting places as well.

When I first became aware of the Indian Marker Tree in Gateway Park in southeast Dallas, it was, as far as I knew, the only Comanche marker tree that was still alive. Visiting the park today, one can imagine Comanche tipis rising up from the grassy land, with the hills on three sides. Those hills are now dappled with suburban homes, but only two hundred years ago they were suitably protected places for Comanche lookouts.

The Marker Pecan in Gateway Park had survived insects, pests, and bulldozers. Still, it was aging and had been through a few difficult years by the time I met there with Glenn Watson, who is a Mystic Warrior of the Lakota and a Pipe Carrier of the Comanche War Scouts. It was memorable to be there as he played haunting

Glenn Watson, Mystic Warrior of the Lakota and Pipe Carrier of the Comanche War Scouts, performed a ritual healing and prayer over the Indian Marker Pecan not very long before the tree died. Says Watson, "In the Indian world, a lot of the tribes believe that we were put here by the Creator to protect the trees, the prairies, and the animals and to live in harmony and balance with them. This is hard to do when we're less than one-half of one percent of the people—it's a lot of work for such a small group of people."

Watson attempted to heal the badly damaged area of the tree. He used a sage wand in his ritual, covering his body with the smoke, including the soles of his feet, and moving the burning wand around the tree, especially the most damaged area. After thoroughly enveloping the tree with sage smoke, Watson offered ritual spiritual expression, playing his three carved flutes and, in conclusion, saying this brief prayer: "This tree, very special to the Comanche people and to all the Indian people, is a reminder, Father God, that we are the keepers of this country and the environment."

spiritual melodies on his hand-carved cedar flute and said prayers of thanksgiving for the tree.

The Marker Pecan is dead now, but it's almost as if it waited patiently for the final admirers to find it. It produced one very strong last batch of pecans, enough for us to harvest and begin to grow offspring from this tree, one of the last brave participants in life as it used to be. Once the tree was dead, we were able to examine the trunk, and we found it to be even older than we thought: at least three hundred years old. It had seen many, many changes, this tree. And unlike many of the Comanche who camped beneath its boughs, it was born where the wind blew free and there was nothing to break the light of the sun. And there it proudly stood until the day it died.

This is one of those stories whose ending makes me proud to be in this line of work. When the offspring of this tree are large enough, we will plant one in Gateway Park, right next to the Marker Pecan that stood sentry for so many centuries. When it reaches the correct height, descendants of the Comanche who camped here will help stake it down in the traditional growing shape of a marker tree.

THE PECAN

Pecan trees (*Carya illinoensis*) are indigenous to the U.S. Southlands, and they were much used and highly prized by Indian tribes; in fact, there were often tribal laws to protect these trees, whose nuts were used for protein-rich food and whose shells were an ingredient in long-lasting dyes. As settlers arrived, they too appreciated the tree, and today the South is pecan country, known for pecan pies, pralines, and roasted nuts.

The tree has long root structures and needs a good water supply to grow to its full height of up to one hundred feet. It's a slow-growing tree, however, and it will be only about fifteen to twenty feet tall after ten years. The tree fruits abundantly in the South, and although this tree is not known for doing well in the North, there are varieties of pecan trees that produce a fine, filtered shade in northern locations. When planted from seed, the trees bear their first pecan crops in four to seven years, the crops becoming lush and heartier for several years thereafter. Pecans drop to the ground when ripe, so it isn't even necessary to use ladders for the harvest. The leaves of the pecan tree are enormous, often twelve to eighteen inches long, and they turn bright gold in the fall.

How to Grow a Pecan from Seed

OCTOBER: Gather the fruit, which is a nut one to two inches long, from a pecan tree. The nut is round or oval to pear-shaped and covered in a thick husk. The husk is green at first, turning dark brown to black as the nut ripens and the husk dries out. The best method for harvesting is to gather the nuts after they drop on the ground. At this point the husk will be completely dried and will be separating from the nutshell. The actual seed lies protected within the hard nutshell. Each nut contains one seed; for ten to twenty trees, gather twenty to forty nuts.

Fortunately, nuts were collected from the Indian Marker Pecan before it was lost to old age.

❧ Remove any remaining pieces of dried husk from the nutshell, taking care not to break the shell. Next place the nuts in a large, resealable plastic bag. In a large bowl, thoroughly moisten three cups of coarse-grade perlite with three cups of water. With a slotted spoon, add the drained perlite to the seeds in the bag and lightly toss to thoroughly mix the seeds with the perlite. Mark the date on the bag, seal it tight, and put it in the vegetable storage bin of the refrigerator at a temperature setting of 40° to 44°F. The seeds will need to remain in the refrigerator for thirty to ninety days.

❧ Check the seeds every second week, looking for mold. If mold appears, rinse the seeds in a solution of ten parts water to one part household bleach and mix with a new batch of perlite in a new plastic bag, dated with the original date.

JANUARY: By this time the nuts should have been in refrigeration for thirty to ninety days, and it is time to transfer them to three- or four-inch planting trays filled with loose potting soil. Remove the seeds from the perlite and place them on the soil surface in rows two to three inches apart, then cover with half an inch of soil.

❧ Place the trays in an area protected from freezing, with lots of sunlight and temperatures from 72° to 85°F. Use a water-misting bottle to keep the soil just moist. Once the tiny sprouts begin to emerge, incorporate a liquid fertilizer at one-quarter strength every other watering, and spray weekly with a fungicide to prevent mildew.

MAY: When the seedlings are two to three inches tall, carefully transplant each one to an individual three- or four-quart growing pot filled with potting soil. After five days, add liquid fertilizer at the recommended strength and fertilize once a week.

AUGUST: When the seedlings reach a height of fifteen inches and the trunks are pencil-thick, plant them in the ground. For planting instructions, see page 118.

WHERE TO PLANT YOUR PECAN

Pecans, even more than most other trees, need good, deep, moist topsoil to thrive. That is why they do so well in the South along creek bottoms. If you have appropriate topsoil, choose a place in your yard where the tree will get plenty of sun and where the roots will have room to grow.

To get the best nut production, I feed my trees in the early spring with slow-release fertilizer. This allows the tree plenty of food to produce a tasty and outstanding crop.

2
BERKELEY PLANTATION SYCAMORE

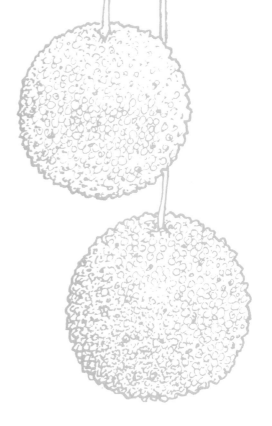

ON A SULTRY SUMMER evening in July 1862, Robert Ellicombe, a captain in the Union Army, was deeply disturbed by the moans of a wounded soldier who lay in the strip of land that separated the Confederate and Union forces near Berkeley Plantation in Virginia. Captain Ellicombe decided it was his duty as a human being to bring the suffering man in for medical attention, even though doing so meant risking his own life. Snipers were active on both sides, and anything that moved in the dark was a fair target.

Crawling cautiously on his stomach, Ellicombe finally reached the wounded man. He could tell it was a very young Confederate soldier, but his resolve didn't waver. Tugging as carefully as possible, Ellicombe began the arduous task of pulling the soldier back behind Union lines. Unfortunately, the young man didn't make it; he died before Ellicombe could get him to safety.

Ellicombe placed the body in a trench, then called for a lantern so he could determine the soldier's identity. Suddenly the captain went cold with shock. In the dim light, he recognized the face of his own son! The boy, whose dream it was to be a composer, had been studying music in the South and, without telling his parents, had left school to join the Confederate army.

The grief-stricken father was given special permission to give his son, though an enemy soldier, a military burial behind Union lines. As a final farewell to his beloved boy, he asked the company bugler to play a short piece of music written on a scrap of paper by the dead boy and found in the pocket of his uniform. The notes on that piece of paper were the music of "Taps."

All of the facts that we know about the origins of this famous tune—that it was handwritten on a scrap of paper given to a bugler named Fisk by Ellicombe's commanding general at Berkeley Plan-

COMMON NAME: SYCAMORE
SCIENTIFIC NAME: *Platanus occidentalis*
AKA: American plane tree, buttonwood, lacewood

tation during that very month—support this story, and it wouldn't surprise me at all if it were true.

Berkeley Hundred Plantation in Virginia has been called the ancestral home of all Americans. On December 4, 1619, thirty-eight travel-weary English settlers fell to their knees in prayers of thanksgiving here, nearly a year before the Pilgrims reached Plymouth. Two years later these same settlers distilled America's first bourbon. But several months after that the small colony was wiped out in an Indian massacre.

Not surprisingly, this dampened the enthusiasm of the land's owner, John Smythe, who had remained in England and was a partner in the Virginia Company, which had been established to raise tobacco and "tame" portions of the new American wilderness. Because Smythe chose not to keep the land (his "Berkeley one hundred" acres) a working facility, it reverted to the English government, and small farmers took over various parcels of it.

Meanwhile, a young Englishman named Benjamin Harryson (later changed to Harrison) had emigrated to the new land. Though of humble origins, he had enough education to become the clerk of the local council and to be elected to Virginia's House of Burgesses the next year. Although originally a man of no means, he had a head for business, and by 1634 he was able to buy two hundred acres of land. He married, and shortly after his wife bore a son, Benjamin Harrison II, the elder Benjamin died. However, his

Berkeley Plantation in Charles City, Virginia, built in 1720, is the oldest three-story brick building in the country.

THE SYCAMORE is a tree that you can plant and grow across a wide range of American climates and landscapes because the tree has proven its flexibility in this regard. For instance, the sycamore is not a genuine species of the prairie, but it has made a long march across the Plains states, playing a starring role in the long-standing, dramatic conflict between the tallgrass prairie and eastern deciduous forest biomes. The shifts in this historic struggle are determined by long-term rainfall patterns—extended wet cycles enable the trees to move westward, while dry years give a leg up to the prairie grasses. In the river valleys, the trees have an added advantage thanks to extra moisture, which is why the woodlands extend onto the plains in slight but distinct fingers of forest.

The sycamore has come to so enjoy rich river soils that in the Mississippi and Ohio River valleys they may grow to spectacular heights of 175 feet and circumferences of 14 feet, and they may live for more than five hundred years.

talent for entrepreneurship was obviously inherited, and Benjamin II was able to expand the family holdings even in difficult financial times. By the age of fifteen, Benjamin II and his half-brother were running a five-hundred-acre plantation.

Each successive generation of Benjamin Harrisons married higher into society. Benjamin III was the son who acquired Berkeley Plantation in 1691, across the river from his father's holdings, while his younger brothers, Nathaniel and Henry, kept the original acreage between them.

Thus the Harrison clan became one of the first true American dynasties, and Berkeley became its family seat. In 1726, Benjamin Harrison IV built the first three-story brick house on American soil. (The house still stands today, a fine example of early Georgian architecture.) His son, Benjamin Harrison V, who signed the Declaration of Independence, was born here, as was *his* son, William Henry Harrison.

William Henry Harrison—known as "Old Tippecanoe" after his legendary battle at the Tippecanoe River with Chief Tecumseh—was elected the ninth president of the United States in 1841. President Harrison caught pneumonia during his lengthy outdoor inaugural address, and within the month claimed an unfortunate "first," becoming the first president to die in office.

No one is certain when the Berkeley Plantation Sycamore, a stately old tree that stands near the plantation's main dock on the James River, was planted. We know it was already full-grown in

1862 when Abraham Lincoln came ashore from the James River to review and encourage the Army of the Potomac under its boughs; General George McClellan had regrouped his troops at Berkeley Plantation after the Seven Days battles. During that summer the haunting melody "Taps" was first played under the sycamore. The stories this tree could tell!

One of my most memorable experiences took place because of a sycamore. In 1991 Russia was going to celebrate its first May Day as a democracy. Instead of its customary military parade, the Russians wanted the holiday to emphasize peace. The Voice of America radio station held a contest to choose the best gift for the United States to send to this historic parade.

I, of course, suggested we send a historic tree as a symbol of peace. To my happy surprise, my entry won the contest. I was asked to fly to Russia to present the tree and to help plant it at the Russian White House in Moscow, and I was excited to do so.

The tree I chose was the White Plains Sycamore, a descendant of the tree that George Washington had camped under at his White Plains, New York, headquarters. The sycamore was an especially good choice because it does well in northern climates such as Russia's.

The tree itself was fifteen feet tall. We had clearance from the U.S. and Russian governments to export and import the tree. Because of strict agricultural regulations, however, we couldn't take any soil! For the trip we had to completely wash off the roots and pack the tree in a coffinlike contraption with moss surrounding the root ball.

At the end of April 1991 I boarded the Aeroflot flight to Moscow. Everything went smoothly until the plane taxied to a stop at the Moscow Airport. Suddenly the intercom crackled to life: "Is Jeff Meyer on board? We are looking for Jeff Meyer!"

What could I do? I identified myself, and before anyone else unbuckled his seatbelt, I was escorted up the aisle to two armed guards who stood impassively awaiting me. I'd be lying if I told you I wasn't nervous. In fact, I was terrified, picturing the news reports back home: *U.S. citizen last seen on airplane between two soldiers carrying machine guns. He claimed he was only a tree guy!*

Once we were off the plane, they took me around to the back of the airplane, where the tree was being unloaded. I realized then that I was supposed to be a witness to this, along with a small crowd of people: my interpreter, my chauffeur, and my military escort. I was being treated like a head of state! The sycamore and I had a very colorful ride into Moscow, complete with entourage and military flags flying.

GREEK SMART

The name "sycamore" comes from the Greek sykomoros, *a type of fig tree native to the Mediterranean. Some leaf similarities seem to have caused this name transference. It is believed that true sycamore trees were held sacred in ancient Egypt and are the first trees represented in Egyptian art.*

The next two days were a whirlwind of meeting and greeting, but nothing matched the day of the parade. On May 1, I planted the tree on the grounds of the Russian White House, next to the Kremlin. I was flanked by U.S. General Patrick Brady, who was president of the U.S. Medal of Honor Society; by Alexander Reuskoy, then vice president of Russia; and by Jay Pieffer, from West Penn Power Company, and Kevin McCarthy, who had sponsored the tree-planting contest. After the greatest pomp surrounding any tree planting I've been involved with, that same august group of men and I were taken to the front of the May Day Parade, where we marched with the U.S. flag through Moscow to Lenin's tomb. We were led up the stairs to the top of the tomb, which now served as a parade reviewing station. We watched the parade with Russia's top generals, who passed shots of vodka with pickle chasers back and forth in great merriment the whole time.

Later I was presented with white ash seeds from the Russian White House, crab apple seeds that had traveled to space on *Sputnik,* and seeds from the Tolstoy White Birch. It was absolutely thrilling.

My other fond memory of the sycamore is a bit more all-American. I remember when Forest, my older boy, began to play baseball and I, of course, became a baseball dad. The only problem was there was no shade at all near that ball field—or, more to my discomfort—near the bleachers. All the parents sat there, watching our boys of summer and roasting in that blazing sun.

Given my work with trees, it was only a matter of time before I was struck with the idea of planting ten sycamore saplings near the bleachers. Ten or eleven years later, both of my boys are still playing ball—and Anne and I join the other parents in shaded comfort under spreading sycamores that are now thirty feet tall and twenty feet wide. It has made a giant difference in our enjoyment of the game!

The Sycamore

I love sycamores (*Platanus occidentalis*); they grow into large trees that fling their branches open, yet they're irregular, each one unique. In a way they reflect the spirit of Americans: at our best we're open and adventurous, but we are also as different from one another as we can possibly be.

Sycamores can grow to heights of 50 to 150 feet; for sheer massive size, no other tree in the eastern half of the United States comes close. Sycamores are wonderful generational trees. If you

plant one now, you can have every expectation it will flourish for five hundred or six hundred years. Talk about witnesses to history!

Sycamores have a mottled brown bark that is papery thin and will flake off to reveal a whitish underbark. The leaves are shaped rather like a tent with side poles. The trees bear small flowers in spring and have small, round, inedible fruits that last through the winter.

The wood of these sturdy trees is hard and coarse-grained. Long before the colonists arrived, Native Americans used sycamores for dugout canoes. The massive size of the trees made it possible to have very long canoes—one was reportedly sixty-five feet long and weighed nine thousand pounds! In colonial times, sycamores were popular for practical items such as crates and barrels, as well as for furniture and cabinets.

Today these beauties are being planted purposefully in America's cities. Thanks to their size, the shade of their branches cools the air by several important degrees, giving respite to those outside and necessitating less ozone-depleting air-conditioning inside. Sycamores can also recycle a huge amount of carbon dioxide into fresh oxygen. They do wonders for the air quality of their city homes. Next time you stroll past one soaking up car emissions on a city street, you might murmur a word of thanks.

HOW TO GROW A SYCAMORE FROM SEED

NOVEMBER: Gather fruits from the sycamore tree. The fruits first appear on the tree as one- to one-and-a-half-inch green balls, which will turn brown as they mature. They can be harvested anytime after this transformation. The ball itself is made up of multiple seeds, which are only three-quarters of an inch long and less than a quarter of an inch wide. The portion of the seed closest to the center of the fruit is pointed and hard, and gradually fans out into a hairy tuft. To grow ten to twenty trees you will need only one or two balls, as each ball contains at least twenty seeds.

❧ Place the balls in an open container set in the sun to dry for one to two days. Once they're completely dry you'll be able to easily dislodge the seeds from the fruit ball with firm pressure.

❧ Separate the seeds by continuing to break the ball apart and rubbing each seed until it separates from the ones surrounding it. (The rubbing also will remove the hairy tuft, which is unnecessary

TRUNKMATES

Raccoons, possums, squirrels, and wood ducks make happy homes in the trunk cavities and major branches of the sycamore, while the sprawling, open branches of the older sycamores house impressive nests of great blue herons.

for the planting process.) The most important portion of the seed is the hard, pointy tip. Place the seeds in a large, resealable plastic bag. In a large bowl, mix three cups of coarse-grade perlite with three cups of water so that it is thoroughly moist. With a slotted spoon, add the drained perlite to the seeds in the bag and lightly toss to thoroughly mix the seeds with the perlite. Mark the date on the bag, seal it tight, and put it in the vegetable storage bin of the refrigerator at a temperature setting of 40° to 44°F. The seeds will need to remain in the refrigerator for sixty to ninety days.

FEBRUARY: After the seeds have been in refrigeration for sixty to ninety days, it is time to transfer them to planting trays three to four inches deep filled with loose potting soil. Remove the seeds from the perlite and place them on the soil surface in rows two to three inches apart, then cover with one-quarter inch of soil.

❧ Place the trays in an area protected from freezing, with lots of sunlight and temperatures from 72° to 85°F. Use a water-misting bottle to keep the soil moist. Once the tiny sprouts begin to emerge, incorporate a liquid fertilizer at one-quarter strength for every other watering, and spray weekly with a fungicide to prevent mildew.

MARCH (OR AFTER THE LAST FROST): When the seedlings are two to three inches tall, carefully transplant each one to an individual three- or four-quart growing pot filled with potting soil. After five days, use liquid fertilizer at the recommended strength once a week.

AUGUST: When the seedlings reach a height of fifteen inches and the trunks are pencil-thick, plant them in the ground. For planting instructions, see page 118.

(Top) Seed balls from the Berkeley Plantation Sycamore are shipped to our nursery in Jacksonville, and each tiny seed is separated from the balls.

(Middle) Germinated seedlings are planted in starter trays while the roots develop.

(Bottom) The seedlings are grown in the trays until they are ready to be planted outdoors.

Where to Plant Your Sycamore

I like to think of sycamores as sun lovers; they enjoy a location where they can spread their branches and soak up the sun. They are hearty trees and will thrive in a wide range of soil conditions, in wet or dry soil. (If the ground is too dry, buy a bag of potting soil and add it to the planting area to add natural moisture.) These seedlings can be planted successfully from Florida to Minnesota. Sycamores are truly trees for all seasons.

3
GEORGE WASHINGTON
TULIP POPLAR

WHILE JOHN ADAMS had always yearned to be president of the United States, George Washington wanted nothing more than to be a farmer. It had always irked Adams that Washington, whom he felt he had created by championing him as commander in chief of the fledgling country's army, became the popular, two-term first president. Even during Adams's own inaugural, as Washington was stepping down, it appeared that George got the better of him. "He seemed," Adams complained to his wife, "to enjoy a triumph over me. Methought I heard him say, 'Ay! I'm fairly out and you fairly in. See which of us will be happiest!'"

And it was true. George Washington, the tall Virginian who embraced the life of a wilderness fighter, followed his beliefs onto the battlefield as a military officer and only grudgingly accepted the call to public office. He wrote almost ecstatically to his close friend the marquis de Lafayette, "At last, my dear Marquis, I am become a private citizen on the banks of the Potomac, and under the shadow of my own vine and own fig tree."

For Washington, above all, loved the outdoors. When he was eleven his father died, and he became a ward of his half-brother, Lawrence, who owned a beautiful estate in Virginia. It was a blessing in some ways for the boy, who had at best a spotty education. Lawrence, well educated in England, had a distinguished career in the Royal Navy under Admiral Vernon (for whom he renamed his estate) and had married the refined and lovely Anne Fairfax. Under Lawrence's tutelage, Washington's education truly began. He enjoyed tales of his brother's military exploits, took eagerly to the pursuits of the gentry (including dancing, horseracing, and card playing), and most of all became an enthusiastic pupil of agriculture and farming.

COMMON NAME: TULIP POPLAR
SCIENTIFIC NAME: *Liriodendron tulipifera*
AKA: tulip tree, yellow poplar
STATE TREE: Indiana, Kentucky, Tennessee

OLD BARK

One of the oldest species of tree, the tulip poplar goes back around 50 million years, making it truly prehistoric. Its lineage can be traced to the ancient magnolias, and fossil leaves have been discovered in rock deposits in Europe.

General Washington
at Princeton, in a
portrait by the
American painter
John Trumbull.

Since his youth he had had a special affinity for trees, although, no, he did *not* chop down a cherry tree. So little was actually known of Washington's boyhood that Reverend Weems, an early biographer, invented this legend to fill in the gaps. The good reverend thought it illustrated Washington's great respect for the truth.

Washington's first real job, at age sixteen, was as an assistant surveyor for Lord Fairfax's 5 million acres in the Northern Neck and the Shenandoah Valley. To read Washington's journals of the trip, one would suppose he was on a tree-spotting expedition; every day he took great pains to list and enthuse over each variety of tree they saw.

In 1752, Lawrence died, and his only surviving child, Sarah, died two months later. Thus Washington became, at age twenty, the manager and eventual owner of one of Virginia's loveliest estates. His years of apprenticeship with Lawrence and his own natural inclinations toward agriculture served him very well. He added to the original estate until it exceeded 8,000 acres and explored all the newest farming techniques, including crop rotation and fertilizing with silt from the bottom of the Potomac. When he married Martha Dandridge Custis, she brought him both the qualities of a good hostess and another 15,000 acres.

As we know, Washington's life as a farmer had to come second to such concerns as the French and Indian War, the Revolutionary War, and the presidency of the United States. But home was where his heart was, and he always returned as quickly as possible.

One of his greatest joys at Mount Vernon was the role of landscape architect. He enlarged the main house and designed the rolling lawn in front of it—a formal bowling green—facing westward, the direction in which he firmly believed his nation's future was heading.

Along each side of the bowling green he planted long rows of trees, choosing each variety carefully and running serpentine paths in and out of the shade of the trees. More than a decorative planting, the trees and paths provided a pleasant pastime for the many guests the Washingtons entertained. Even before he was president, George and Martha entertained hundreds of guests a year, most of whom were at least invited to dinner, if not to spend the night. One year Washington's diary noted only two evenings when the family dined alone—both times during blizzards.

The custom of the day meant Washington rose before the sun, saw to the plantation, had dinner at the early hour of three o'clock, and entertained his guests until bedtime at nine o'clock.

Since there was no air-conditioning in those days, the evening's entertainment was often centered outdoors, and many of George's happiest and most productive hours were spent walking with guests in the shade of the trees on the bowling green. What great philosophical treatises did Washington discuss with his close friends Thomas Jefferson, Ben Franklin, or the marquis de Lafayette? From their letters and journals we know that it's completely likely they were discussing trees! Each of these men was an avid horticulturist. As a matter of fact, Washington, Jefferson, Franklin, and John Bartram, the king's horticulturist, had a program to swap seeds from their best trees with each other.

Washington especially loved the tulip poplar; he planted two himself in the august tree line on his bowling green. The marquis de Lafayette also loved the tulip poplar; he felt it was a quintessential American tree, and he took saplings home to France as a thank-you from the fledgling country for French help in the recent revolution. Lafayette took the trees to Versailles to be planted and gave one personally to Marie Antoinette.

The tulip poplars that George Washington planted are still alive and growing at Mount Vernon today. Like Washington himself, they are stately, impressive, and tall—over one hundred feet tall. These national treasures were the trees that originally inspired the Famous & Historic Trees project. Wouldn't it be wonderful, we thought, if we could grow direct descendants of these Mount Vernon tulip poplars? So we gathered seeds and planted them. And nothing happened. We tried again for a couple of years. Nothing. Finally Dr. Frank Santamour, the tree geneticist of the National Arboretum, figured out the problem. The trees had grown so tall that their blossoms were eighty to one hundred feet off the ground—much too high for bees to reach to complete the pollination.

So Dr. Santamour suggested that we get a cherry picker to carry him up to hand-pollinate the seeds. At the end of the season, we harvested them, planted them, and waited with bated breath. Finally we had direct descendants of Washington's tulip poplars.

The flowers of a full-grown tulip poplar grow so high in the tree that they can rarely be seen from the ground. A second- or third-story window is a better viewing site.

Dr. Frank Santamour brought some fertile pollen from a tulip poplar in the National Arboretum, then rode up in a cherry picker to hand-pollinate the flowers of George Washington's tree at Mount Vernon.

The tulip-shaped blossom of the tulip poplar is quite beautiful, ranging in color from greenish yellow to a deep orange. Unfortunately for mere mortals, the blossoms are found high in the tree canopy, which may begin thirty or fifty feet up the tree. With nearly a teaspoon of nectar in every flower, the blossoms are favorites of the pollinating honeybees, ants, and other high-flying nectar-lovers. Luckily for the earthbound creatures, after the flower petals disappear, the seeded cone falls to the ground during autumn and winter, providing more than a few square meals for squirrels, rabbits, robins, blue jays, bobwhites, and others.

We have manually pollinated this tree a few times since the first pollination in 1989, each outing producing good seed crops. The tulip poplar cannot be grown from cuttings, so we take great care every time we undertake the manual pollination process. Because this tree holds such special interest for me, I did something unusual with the first batch of the offspring. Usually we sell all the small saplings, but with this tree I kept forty to grow into large trees at my own nursery to plant on special historic occasions.

Descendants of Washington's original trees have already done their parents proud. One was returned to George Washington's home at Mount Vernon. I've planted a large Washington Tulip Poplar on the grounds of the Naval Observatory in Washington, D.C., where the country's vice president lives. Yet another thrives on the grounds of Florida's state capital in Tallahassee.

In the winter of 1999, the last of the tulip poplars that the marquis de Lafayette took to Versailles as a gift to Marie Antoinette was killed by a violent windstorm. It made me proud to offer a descendant of those Mount Vernon trees to replace it—the links of history and friendship between Lafayette and Washington, between France and the United States, may now continue for generations to come.

The Tulip Poplar

The tulip poplar (*Liriodendron tulipifera*) is more closely related to the magnolia than to the true poplar. It is a tall, straight, handsome tree with branches that often angle up as though lifting hands to the sky; full grown, it's an inspiring sight. The bark is light gray. The large, tulip-shaped flowers are orange and green and usually blossom in May or June. If you crush the leaves and buds, they smell spicy and aromatic. The leaves are distinctive; they are notch-tipped with four points. In fact, the whole tree is distinctive; once you know what it looks like, it fairly jumps out at you and is not easily mistaken for any other tree.

Wood from tulip poplars is straight-grained and won't split easily, which makes it useful for making furniture, shingles, boats, pulp, and toys. Its seeds are popular food for squirrels and songbirds. A stately addition to any landscape, the tulip poplar is notoriously difficult to grow from seed. Even in our nursery, which has optimal growing conditions, we plant 50 to 100 seeds for every tree that grows. (The saplings are much easier to grow, and, as you know, we do sell them.) I'm not saying that planting them from seed isn't worth the trouble—in fact, there's nothing quite as satisfying as that eventual success.

How to Grow a Tulip Poplar from Seed

November: Gather the fruits from a tulip poplar tree. The cone-shaped fruits appear at the ends of the branches, falling to the ground in autumn. The oval to pear-shaped fruit is made up of several flat seeds, one and a half inches long and one-half inch wide. The cones can easily be harvested from the tree once they are tan, with very little green remaining. Tulip poplars do not typically germinate very well, so it may take as many as five hundred seeds to yield five seedlings.

❧ Once the fruits have been harvested, they should be laid out on a flat surface in a warm, dry room and left to dry completely. When completely dry, the seeds will be papery to the touch and can easily be pulled from the cone by hand. At this point, place the dry seeds in a large, resealable plastic bag. In a large bowl, mix three cups of coarse-grade perlite with three cups of water so that it is thoroughly moist. With a slotted spoon, add the drained per-

lite to the bag and lightly toss to thoroughly mix the seeds with the perlite. Mark the date on the bag, seal it tight, and put it in the vegetable storage bin of the refrigerator at a temperature setting of 40° to 44°F. The seeds will need to remain in the refrigerator for sixty to ninety days.

❧ Check the seeds every second week, looking for mold. If mold appears, rinse the seeds in a ten-to-one solution of water and household bleach, mix with a new batch of moist perlite, and re-seal in a new plastic bag, dated with the original date.

FEBRUARY: By now the seeds should have been in refrigeration between sixty and ninety days, and it is time to transfer them to planting trays two to three inches deep filled with loose potting soil. Remove the seeds from the perlite and place them on the soil surface in rows two to three inches apart, then cover with a quarter inch of soil.

❧ Place the trays in an area protected from freezing, with lots of sunlight and temperatures from 72° to 85°F. Use a water-misting bottle to keep the soil just moist. Once the tiny sprouts begin to emerge, incorporate a liquid fertilizer at one-quarter strength for every other watering, and spray weekly with a fungicide to prevent mildew.

IT'S A STATE THING

As one of the most favored trees in the eastern United States, the tulip poplar was bound to become the state tree in at least one of the states in which it is (or was) abundant. Indeed, the state of Indiana adopted the tulip poplar as state tree in 1931 as a reference to a time when forests plentiful with the species covered most of the state. The destruction of Indiana's forests is symbolized on the state seal by a woodsman felling a tree; the seal also portrays a tulip poplar leaf.

The tulip poplar is also the state tree of Kentucky and of Tennessee, which chose it because of its extensive use by Tennessee pioneers in building houses, barns, and other farm buildings. And Pennsylvania came *this close* to adopting the tulip poplar as state tree in 1929, also in deference to its extensive use in dwelling and boat construction, as well as for cabinetwork, household items, and decorative purposes. But Pennsylvania ultimately rejected this choice when a purist (or nitpicker, as the case may be) pointed out that the tulip poplar is rarely seen in northern Pennsylvania; the state adopted the western hemlock instead.

The tulip poplar is exceeded in popularity as a state tree only by the sugar maple, which represents New York, Vermont, West Virginia, and Wisconsin.

MAY: When the seedlings are two to three inches tall, carefully transplant each one to an individual three- or four-quart growing pot with potting soil. After five days, incorporate the liquid fertilizer at the recommended strength and fertilize once a week.

AUGUST: Tulip poplar seedlings are relatively slow growing, so it is best to keep them in a controlled environment until they have lived through their first winter and have demonstrated good growth. When the seedlings reach a height of fifteen inches and the trunks are pencil-thick, plant them in the ground. For planting instructions, see page 118.

WHERE TO PLANT YOUR TULIP POPLAR

As mentioned, this tree is hard to grow from seed, but whether you're growing from seed or sapling, make certain your soil is fertile and moist. A location near a lake, pond, or other body of water is a perfect setting for this picturesque tree and will provide continuous moisture. Plant out in the open where there is plenty of sun. The tulip poplar grows at a good pace, and once started it will be a great shade tree for your yard.

A tulip poplar seedling ready to be planted outdoors.

4
Patrick Henry
Osage Orange

THE MOLDING AND SHAPING of public opinion has changed significantly through the years. These days a successful politician is one who knows how to manipulate the media and talk in thirty-second sound bites. It's also been a given for many decades now that a president's—or senator's—speeches are in all likelihood written for him by pundits and professional speech-writers.

But in Lincoln's day, folks would come from all over to hear a noted speaker hold forth for hours and consider it a great after-noon's entertainment. People had tremendous respect for the gift of oratory.

Back in the eighteenth century, the Winston family was known for having this gift. The story goes that after General Brad-dock's terrible defeat during the French and Indian War, the sol-diers were hungry, ragged, and freezing—ready, to a man, to desert and run. It was then that William Winston, a young lieutenant, mounted a tree stump and addressed them with stirring words and great fire about liberty and patriotism.

"Let us march on! Lead us against the enemy!" the men cried together when he was done. Said one eyewitness, "So forceful was his speech that the recruits were now anxious to meet the dangers which shortly before had almost produced a mutiny."

Apparently Billy Winston's nephew Patrick inherited this ora-torical gift. It was a good thing he did. Young Patrick Henry had very little formal education, and he was not a great reader. (He was, by all reports, a champion at fishing, able to sit still under a shady tree for hours, awaiting a bite. He was also quite a prankster, likely to strip off his clothes and dive into the water so quickly that his companions in a canoe would get totally soaked when he over-

COMMON NAME: OSAGE ORANGE
SCIENTIFIC NAME: *Maclura pomifera*
AKA: hedge apple, bodark

turned it.) These abilities did not help him make a living. Henry failed at two businesses and was running through his wife's dowry; when the children started coming, he realized he had to find a profession quickly. He had long admired preachers and lawyers for their oratorical skills, and he decided to study for the bar himself. He barely passed (the examiners told him they'd let him pass but he'd better keep studying), but once he was in court, his natural wit and speaking talent made him a great success. He soon became famous in courtrooms throughout Virginia.

Patrick Henry had strong convictions and the ability to give them voice. It's easy to forget that the outcome of the American Revolution was not a foregone conclusion. Virtually all of the colonists involved in government were of English descent; many of them thought that unfair English decisions like the Stamp Act were irritating policies that could be borne and would eventually be reversed by England's Parliament. The idea of totally breaking from their friends and family back in Britain—in fact, waging war on them—was impossible, and the idea of raising an army made up of backwoods colonists was laughable.

Patrick Henry was a delegate to the Second Continental Congress when these issues came to a head. At the meeting in St. John's Church in Richmond, Virginia, on March 23, 1775, several well-respected gentlemen stood to explain why the colonists should continue to have patience and hold on to hope that Parliament would act more favorably, and their point was well taken.

The 400-year-old Patrick Henry Osage Orange, at Red Hill plantation in Virginia, where Henry is buried, is fifty-four feet tall with a span of ninety feet. It is one of the two largest Osage orange trees in the United States.

Patrick Henry was known as the "voice of the American Revolution" for his fiery speeches.

But, like his uncle Billy on that tree stump, Patrick Henry stood up and, with his words alone, changed the course of history. "There is no longer any room for hope," Henry said. "If we wish to be free...we must fight! I repeat it, sir, we must fight! An appeal to arms and to the God of Hosts is all that is left us... Is life so dear, or peace so sweet, as to be purchased at the price of chains and slavery? Forbid it, Almighty God! I know not what course others may take, but as for me, give me liberty or give me death!"

Henry's motion passed by five votes. Those favoring revolution submitted a plan the next morning (in fact, Thomas Jefferson had written it well in advance), and it was adopted; the Continental Army was formed.

Patrick Henry went on to have a distinguished career that included being governor of Virginia five times, both in war and as the first American governor of the state. He was also a very vocal holdout against the Constitution of the United States until the Bill of Rights was added to protect individual freedoms.

But as he grew older, his priorities shifted noticeably. He was a family man, to put it mildly. He had two wives (the first died), fourteen children, and sixty grandchildren! So he began buying land, hoping to leave each of his sons a country estate. As he approached sixty, he bought a plantation called Red Hill in Long Island, Virginia, and moved the family there. Although the land was lush and remarkable, the house was very small. By this time Henry was getting on in years, but he still had six young sons at home, and they had the run of the place. Visitors to Red Hill used to find Henry with "little ones climbing all over him in every direction, or dancing around him with obstreperous mirth, to the tune of his violin, while the only contest seemed to be who should make the most noise."

Osage orange trees are native to the lower Mississippi Valley and were not known in Virginia until Lewis and Clark brought cuttings back from their journeys. After Henry's death at the age of sixty, Lewis and Clark gave his daughter an Osage orange tree, which she immediately planted at Red Hill.

In 1990, Rick Crouse, my friend at American Forests, introduced me to one of the most magnificent trees in the United States, none other than this very same Osage orange. By then, it was one of the two largest Osage oranges in the country. What a grand tree it is! Huge and rambling, it's well known throughout the region and certainly well remembered by anyone who has seen it. Rick took cuttings from it, and I remember seeing photos of them packed in coolers before being shipped to my nursery in Florida. It was very satisfying when they rooted and grew tall. It's become one of my favorite trees.

THE OSAGE ORANGE

I admit that when I was a boy, my appreciation of the Osage orange (*Maclura pomifera*) was not exactly what you'd call sophisticated. These trees grew along fence lines all over Iowa, and in the fall, when the large, round, inedible fruits, called hedge apples, fell from the trees, we kids loved to play ball and toss them around. They made a very satisfying splat when they hit the ground. My mother, of course, had other uses for the fruits. She would slice them much like oranges and add them to decorative centerpieces, which were, indeed, very lovely.

The Osage orange was unknown in the East until Lewis and Clark's expedition; the explorers found it growing in profusion in a small area that included parts of Oklahoma, Missouri, Texas, and Arkansas. It was named "Osage" after a local Native American tribe that used the flexible wood for bows and "orange" after the scent of the fruits when warmed by the sun.

Known variously as the hedge, hedge apple, and bodark tree, it is the only member of its genus—a monotype. Its closest distant cousin is the mulberry. It is easily recognized by its somewhat shiny, lance-shaped leaves and short, thick thorns.

Once the Osage orange was introduced to colonists and pioneers, it became a very popular tree. When the trees were planted closely in a line, the prickly branches made a natural, impassable fence to keep out animals and serve as a windbreak. Advertised as "horse-high, bull-strong, hog-tight," such fences, trimmed down to "horse height," were used in the Plains states to provide boundaries. In fact, it's estimated that 250,000 miles of Osage orange hedgerows still traverse the country.

Osage orange trees have an incredibly dense wood that contains a natural preservative and is therefore impervious to both rot and pests such as termites. This made it great for fence posts and archery bows, especially in the mid-nineteenth century.

While the Patrick Henry Osage Orange is now fifty-four feet tall with a spread of ninety feet, the average for these trees is thirty to thirty-five feet tall with a spread of twenty-five feet. Known even to its ardent fans as picturesque rather than beautiful, the tree becomes very gnarled and dramatic. The simple leaves are thick and shiny, usually three to six inches long, tapering to a pointed tip. In autumn they turn a flaming bright yellow.

THE OLD VIRGINIA CAPITOL.

The reason Rick and I had to take cuttings of the Patrick Henry tree is that Osage oranges are either male or female, and only the female trees bear the large, fleshy fruits sometimes known as mock oranges. These large, heavy, green-yellow, wrinkled balls contain an average of two hundred seeds. (You don't want to be below one when it drops from the tree!) The male is propagated by cuttings, which root easily. The Patrick Henry Osage Orange is male.

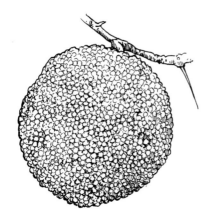

How to Grow an Osage Orange from Seed

OCTOBER: Gather the fruits, which appear as four- to five-inch balls, from the Osage orange tree. The balls are green with dark splotches appearing as they mature. Each ball is made up of multiple fruits, each containing a small, stony seed. To grow ten to twenty trees you will need only one or two balls, for they contain at least two hundred seeds.

The best method of extracting the seeds is to place the fruits in a bucket filled with dead leaves, making sure the bucket has drainage holes. Place the bucket outside, preferably in a partly shady area, out of sight, but exposed to the elements. This will allow the fruits to continue to ripen and eventually rot. After two or three months the fruits should be very soft and easy to pull apart by hand. Once the individual fruits have been separated, remove the stony seeds from the soft flesh and rinse them thoroughly at least three times.

JANUARY: Place the seeds in an open container in a warm, dry room and leave them to dry for a day or two. Next put them in a large, resealable plastic bag. In a large bowl, mix three cups of coarse-grade perlite with three cups of water. With a slotted spoon, add the drained perlite to the seeds in the bag and lightly toss to thoroughly mix. Mark the date on the bag, seal it tight, and put it in the vegetable storage bin of the refrigerator at a temperature of 40° to 44°F. The seeds will need to remain in the refrigerator for thirty to sixty days.

❧ Check the seeds every second week, looking for mold. If mold appears, rinse the seeds in a ten-to-one solution of water and household bleach, mix with a new batch of moist perlite, and reseal in a new plastic bag, dated with the original date.

MARCH: By now the seeds should have been in refrigeration for thirty to sixty days, and it is time to transfer them to planting trays three to four inches deep filled with loose potting soil. Remove the seeds from the perlite and place them on the soil surface in rows two to three inches apart, then cover with a quarter inch of soil.

⤷ Place the trays in an area protected from freezing, with lots of sunlight and temperatures from 72° to 85°F. Use a water-misting bottle to keep the soil just moist. Once the tiny sprouts begin to emerge, incorporate a liquid fertilizer at one-quarter strength for every other watering, and spray weekly with a fungicide to prevent mildew.

JUNE: When the seedlings are two to three inches tall, carefully transplant each one to an individual three- or four-quart growing pot with potting soil. After five days, incorporate the liquid fertilizer at the recommended strength and fertilize once a week.

AUGUST: When the seedlings reach a height of fifteen inches and the trunks are pencil-thick, plant them in the ground.

How to Propagate by Cuttings

JUNE: Take six- to eight-inch cuttings from the new growth, which is referred to as "softwood," as there is no bark formation. To propagate ten to twenty trees, take twice as many cuttings—this method will yield a success rate of about 40 to 65 percent. Purchase a powdered rooting hormone, such as Rootone or Hormex, from any garden shop. Dip the end of the cutting approximately one inch into the rooting hormone and stick the cutting immediately into a soil mix of approximately one-half potting soil, one-quarter sand, and one-quarter perlite. The soil mix should be three to four inches deep in the seed tray, but do not stick the cutting into the soil any deeper than an inch. Place the tray in an area protected from freezing, with lots of sunlight and temperatures from 72° to 85°F. Use a water-misting bottle two or three times a day to keep the soil moist, but do not allow standing water—and never water late in the day, as wet foliage is prone to fungal infection.

AUGUST: Cuttings should be completely rooted in forty to fifty days and ready to be transplanted into three- or four-quart growing

THE BODARK BONUS

The Osage orange's strong yet limber branches were prized by Native Americans for use in the construction of hunting bows. The common name "bodark" is a variation of the French bois d'arc *or "wood of the bow."*

pots filled with potting soil. When the cuttings reach a height of fifteen inches and the trunks are pencil-thick, plant them in the ground. For planting instructions, see page 118.

Where to Plant Your Osage Orange

The Osage orange was such a popular pioneer tree precisely because it can thrive in almost any kind of soil. Poorly drained, rocky, poor topsoil—the tree is not picky, which makes it perfect for urban settings as well as parched, open landscapes. This tree will adapt to the conditions; it will give you considerably more spread and height out in the open, but it will remain smaller and take up less room if it's planted in rocky city soil.

The Osage orange has shallow roots, which means it will fight with nearby grass and trees for nutrients. Give it a little room of its own at the base if you can. And don't forget to collect the fruits to make decorations: slice each ball into thin discs and dry them in flower shapes.

5
JACKSONVILLE
TREATY LIVE OAK

ONE DAY IN 1984, my wife, Anne, and I decided to indulge in one of our favorite pastimes: going over to Treaty Oak Park here in downtown Jacksonville and having a family picnic under the majestic Treaty Oak, a favorite oasis for many local families. The park is delightful; many people come to the heart of our metropolis, the largest city in Florida, to sit under the leafy boughs that canopy half a city block. Near the St. Johns River, which has been a port of entry to the city for hundreds of years, the property and its centerpiece were donated to the city by Jessie Ball du Pont, the wife of Alfred I. du Pont. Jessie's brother, Edward Ball, was closely allied with Alfred's businesses, including the creation of the Florida National Bank and the railroads that eventually brought tourism to the state. Alfred died in 1935, and Jessie lived in Jacksonville until her death in 1970. She loved helping the people of Florida, making life better for its children, especially, and she thought the Treaty Oak was one of the best gifts she could give the city. I think she was right.

There is something about this sprawling and magnificent live oak tree that inspires awe and reverie. What made this tree and that day in 1984 so special to me? I don't know for certain. Perhaps it was being a new father and having a new appreciation for generations, for the passage of time. As Anne spread our picnic lunch, I remembered seeing tintypes of families much like ours sitting exactly where we sat, one hundred years earlier. Needless to say, the families had changed. The tree, however, looked much the same.

The reason I love history so much isn't because of cold facts printed in musty textbooks; it has more to do with imagination. In my mind's eye that day, I felt I could easily be transported back in time, sitting beneath this same tree, to the days when members of

COMMON NAME: LIVE OAK
SCIENTIFIC NAME: *Quercus virginiana*
STATE TREE: Georgia

Filigree gates mark
the entrance to
Treaty Oak Park
in downtown
Jacksonville.

the Timucuan tribe, northern Florida's most populous native tribe, sat for tribal councils where I now sat. (According to historians, Florida was probably one of the last parts of the Americas to be settled. If it's true that the Indian tribes arrived by crossing the Bering Strait while there was still a land bridge, it's understandable that it took them a while to migrate as far south and east as Florida.) The Timucuans established many villages, each surrounded by a twelve-foot-high wall of tree trunks. Come to think of it, I probably wouldn't have been allowed to sit under this tree, especially if it was used for treaty meetings. The Timucuans had a very rigid class system, and ordinary folks weren't allowed anywhere near goings-on initiated by the chiefs or shamans.

On Easter Sunday, 1513, Ponce de Leon landed twenty-five miles from Jacksonville, ten miles south of Pablo Beach on the Atlantic Ocean, and Spain laid claim to much of Florida's land. Fifty years later, Jean Ribault, France's best seaman and a Huguenot, landed and had a column planted, staking France's rival claim to part of the New World's colonies. Over the next years, the Spanish and French rivalry would turn bloody, until the Spanish Catholic

INDIAN MARKER PECAN

AMERICA'S FAMOUS
AND HISTORIC TREES

ABOVE: *Berkeley Plantation Sycamore*
BELOW: *George Washington Tulip Poplar*

ABOVE: *Patrick Henry Osage Orange*
BELOW: *Lewis and Clark Cottonwood*

Jeff Meyer beside the
JACKSONVILLE TREATY LIVE OAK
with a sapling grown from one of its acorns.

ANDREW
JACKSON
SOUTHERN
MAGNOLIA

WALDEN WOODS RED MAPLE

MARK TWAIN CAVE BUR OAK

JOHNNY APPLESEED RAMBO APPLE

GETTYSBURG
ADDRESS
HONEY
LOCUST

Lincoln's
Gettysburg
Address Site

FREDERICK DOUGLASS
WHITE OAK

WYATT EARP
BLACK WALNUT

JOHN F. KENNEDY
POST OAK

ELVIS PRESLEY PIN OAK

MOON SYCAMORE

explorer Pedro Menendez defeated the French Protestant Ribault and went on to found St. Augustine.

Two and a half centuries later, in 1821, Florida was purchased from Spain by the United States. That same year, the small town of Cow Ford was renamed Jacksonville in honor of Andrew Jackson, the territory's first appointed governor. The state, so close to Georgia, soon became part of the Old South, with as many plantations springing up as the sandy soil would allow. In 1845, Florida became the twenty-seventh state in the union.

By the end of that century, Jacksonville was known as a winter haven for northerners, including members of the infant film industry and the New York Giants. Hotels sprang up and tourism became a major industry, due in large part to the steamer services running across the river.

Indians, Spaniards, Huguenots, New York Giants—all of them must have known this tree well, for it has stood here for three hundred years at least, probably many more. Legend has it that many treaties were signed beneath this gargantuan tree. A marker for generation after generation, it survived the Seminole War and the Civil War, as various groups fought for their rights. It stood mute witness to the terrible Cleveland Fibre Factory fire in 1901, which

Jeff Meyer beside the grand Jacksonville Treaty Live Oak, whose sweeping limbs seem to crawl across the ground.

Scott Meyer standing beside "his" crape myrtle in the Meyers' back yard, following the tradition started with his brother's acorn.

destroyed 2,368 buildings and burned 466 acres, practically leveling Jacksonville. Somehow the tree was spared and became part of the rebuilt town.

To me, the Treaty Live Oak is symbolic of many trees in many communities. We all tend to gravitate in awe to these beautiful markers, and because we do, many occurrences, both notable and mundane, tend to happen beneath them. What happened for us the day that Anne and I picnicked under the Treaty Oak was both notable and mundane. Our son, Forest, just eleven months old and a new walker, wandered back to us with an acorn clenched firmly in his chubby fist. From this an idea was born. Why not plant an offspring of this historic tree in honor of our own offspring? Why not have a descendant of this historic Treaty Oak in our own front yard?

That is exactly what Anne and I did. We took the acorn home, sprouted it, and planted it. What grew from that small seed was more than anyone expected.

Forest is now a teenager and an athlete. He enjoys baseball and loves the outdoors and walking in the woods, just like his dad. Forest's tree is now forty feet tall. When Forest's little brother, Scott, was a youngster, we planted a tree for him too, this one in the back yard. Scott is a bit more dramatic than his brother, his personality more outgoing, and his tree, a crape myrtle, is a little showier too. Each boy knows which tree is "his"; after they grow up and move on, I hope they will come back to Jacksonville, much as I revisit Amana, Iowa. My tree is there, and so are my roots. I hope my boys will feel the same way.

But from that little acorn also germinated the idea of growing descendants of important trees. As I mentioned in the introduction, American Forests already had identified many famous and historic trees. It didn't take a huge leap for me to realize that if I could plant a descendant of the Treaty Live Oak for my child, anyone in the United States could plant his or her own tribute to a relative, friend, or event in much the same way. Step by step, seed by seed, we could change the world for the better. We could plant our own monuments, and then do our best to live lives that are worthy of them.

The Live Oak

The live oak (*Quercus virginiana*) is perhaps the tree most associated with the American Deep South. With its huge trunk and wide-spreading branches, often covered with streamers of Spanish moss, it is at once majestic and fanciful. Although it usually tops out at sixty feet (as the Treaty Live Oak does), its rounded crown can have a spread of more than one hundred feet, with some of its limbs five feet in diameter. Its oblong, leathery, evergreen leaves are distinctive, with a pointed base and rounded tip. The narrow acorns are usually an inch long or less. The bark is dark brown and deeply furrowed.

These days, live oaks are used mostly for shade and landscaping, but in earlier times the sheer mass of their limbs and trunk made them perfect for the ribs of wooden ships. Early in our country's history, preserves of live oaks were set aside for use by the navy. Timber used for the USS *Constitution*—known as "Old Ironsides"—came from a navy preserve of live oaks on St. Catherines Island in Georgia; in fact, the live oak is Georgia's state tree.

This is a tree for warmer climates; it thrives from southern Virginia down through Florida and Texas.

How to Grow a Live Oak from Seed

OCTOBER: Gather the fruits, which are the acorns. They are oblong to oval in shape, green at first, turning tan-brown as they ripen, and topped with a corky overcap that is scaly in appearance. Acorns can be gathered from the tree, but they must be fully ripe, showing no green. The easiest way to harvest them is to collect the acorns from the ground, avoiding those with tiny weevil holes and those that feel hollow. Each fruit contains one seed; for ten to twenty trees, gather thirty to sixty acorns.

✤ Put the acorns in 120° water for ten minutes to destroy any weevils or worms that may be present. Place the acorns in an open container and let them dry completely, which should take only a few days. Then remove the scaly overcap and keep only the acorn, being careful not to puncture the seed coat during this process. Plant the acorns immediately in planting trays three to four inches deep filled with loose potting soil, then cover them with half an inch of soil.

✤ Place the trays in an area protected from freezing, with lots of sunlight and temperatures from 72° to 85°F. Use a water-misting bottle to keep the soil just moist. Once the tiny sprouts begin to emerge, incorporate a liquid fertilizer at one-quarter strength for every other watering, and spray weekly with a fungicide to prevent mildew.

MAY: When the seedlings are two to three inches tall, carefully transplant them to individual three- or four-quart growing pots with potting soil. After five days, incorporate the liquid fertilizer at the recommended strength and fertilize once a week.

AUGUST: When the seedlings reach a height of fifteen inches and the trunks are pencil-thick, plant them in the ground. For planting instructions, see page 118.

Where to Plant Your Live Oak

The live oak loves warm, moist, southern climes. It does best in sunlight with good irrigation. Cold temperatures will kill it, but once it has taken hold in a suitable place it is nearly indestructible. Mistletoe, Spanish moss, and ball moss live in live oaks. In earlier times Spanish moss was used as ticking for pillows and mattresses. It certainly reminds me of the Old South.

Each live oak has its own unique character. It is my favorite tree to grow.

6
LEWIS AND CLARK COTTONWOOD

IF YOU WANT to take a trip across the United States these days, you simply boot up your computer, input your starting address and the address of your destination, and within minutes you have a complete printout of which roads to take and which turns to make. It's hard for us to imagine that, in the great timeline of history, it was the equivalent of only minutes ago that no one knew the shape or the boundaries of the North American continent. The Indians who lived here knew their own territories well, but the expanse of land from Atlantic to Pacific was too vast for any-

COMMON NAME: COTTONWOOD

SCIENTIFIC NAME: *Populus deltoides*

AKA: eastern cottonwood

STATE TREE: Kansas, Nebraska, Wyoming

A painting of a Comanche village by George Catlin. The women are dressing robes and drying meat.

CAPTAIN MERIWETHER LEWIS

CAPTAIN WILLIAM CLARK

one to traverse as a matter of course. Even after European settlers arrived and mapped out the eastern half of the United States, the West loomed uncharted and unknown until Thomas Jefferson picked two explorers and naturalists, Meriwether Lewis and William Clark, to lead an expedition across the Mississippi in 1802. With their band of men and a native guide, Sacajawea, could they make it as far as the land stretched, to another ocean? Could they face the hazards of nature, of wild animals, of perhaps hostile tribes, and return alive?

If you've ever read their journals or a book about Lewis and Clark, you know it was a close call. But Jefferson's faith in them was well placed. They were not only resourceful and brave, consummate direction-finders and mapmakers, their curiosity and sharp-eyed recognition of flora and fauna helped document indigenous plants and animals. In some cases their discoveries changed the American landscape (see Chapter 4 on the Osage orange).

In addition, their interactions with the Indians they encountered on their travels were either productive or at least nonviolent—until almost the end of their journey in 1806. Lewis and Clark had parted with plans to meet after crossing the Marias and Missouri rivers. By July 27, Captain Lewis was only two or three days from his destination, and his party was riding in two groups. Lewis was with two men on a high plain, while a man named Drewer led the rest of the company down in a valley. Suddenly, Captain Lewis came upon fifteen warriors and thirty horses silently watching Drewer from above. (At the time, Lewis was certain that that meant fifteen other men were hiding in the surrounding landscape. It was later discovered that hunting parties such as this one often rode with a double quota of horses so their hunting could continue after one set of horses was exhausted.) Even though the three men on the upper track were badly outnumbered, they felt they had no choice but to meet with the hunters; to yell and alert Drewer would certainly have scared the hunters into an attack.

So Lewis and his men presented themselves as diplomatically as possible. As Lewis handed out expensive trinkets, chatting through an interpreter, he described all the treaties they'd already made with other bands of warriors and found out the location of the main camp. Then they all went down and met with the rest of the men, camped under three cottonwood trees, and smoked the peace pipe. They also discovered through their interpreter that these men belonged to a tribe that was well known for thievery.

This was very worrisome to Lewis, who was so close to a successful return. But their success was dependent upon horses and guns, and almost dearer to him were all the artifacts he had gathered and traded for on this consuming, treacherous journey. He would not let them be stolen. He stayed awake past eleven o'clock, talking with the leader of the group. After all the Indians were asleep, he roused a man named Fields to take the next watch.

The hunters made their move at sunrise. Fields was the only man still awake, and he had gotten a bit careless, leaving his rifle by the fire. The braves grabbed Drewer's and Captain Lewis's rifles, as well as those of Fields and his brother, and then they untied the explorers' horses. They were so quiet that Fields didn't notice what was happening until the braves were making a run for it.

Fields called his brother at once, and they pursued the man who had stolen their rifles. In the scuffle that ensued, Fields stabbed the Indian through the heart with a knife and killed him. At the same time, Drewer wrested his gun away; Lewis, who still had a pistol, yelled to the brave who had stolen his gun to drop it, which he did. Drewer asked permission to start shooting, but Lewis forbade it.

They quickly realized that the rest of the hunting party was trying to leave with their horses. Gunfire was exchanged, and another of the hunters was killed. By the time the skirmish was over, the thieves had gotten away with only one of the explorers' horses.

Lewis and his men knew they had to flee. Their lives were in serious danger. The thieves would doubtless be back for horses, rifles, booty, and revenge. They broke camp immediately and pushed their horses to ascend the hills, riding hard. Eight miles from their camp, they crossed a river they named "Battle" after the morning's events. By three o'clock they had reached the Rose River. They'd now come sixty-three miles, so they rested for an hour and a half before pushing on another seventeen miles. They killed a buffalo for food but stopped for only two hours.

By continuing to ride through the night, they reached the river crossing where they expected to find a message from Clark. As it turned out, he'd already passed, and was only a day or so ahead of them. When they reached the shelter of a fort, they finally felt safe.

Historians think this long day was quite significant because it presented the most immediate danger the exploration team ever faced. For years the exact location of the fight was a matter of conjecture. In 1963, Mrs. Helen B. West, the archives assistant of the Museum of the Plains Indians, along with two Boy Scout officials, decided to use the landmarks in Lewis's journal—and the invention of the airplane—to discover the site.

The original
Lewis and Clark
Cottonwood in
Cutbank, Montana,
photographed from
a helicopter.

It took several months, but they were ultimately successful. The locations of the rivers and the bluffs all made sense. And, most amazingly, the three cottonwoods where the men had camped still stood exactly as they had nearly two hundred years earlier.

If before I learned about this place I did not fully appreciate what Lewis and Clark achieved and the hardships they endured, I certainly do now. To say it's a remote location is putting it mildly. Even today, the campsite is seventy miles from the nearest road. The countryside is still unspoiled and wild. When we sent foresters in to collect seeds, they had to go by snowmobile. When we decided to feature it in the PBS special on famous and historic trees, the camera crew had to be flown in by helicopter.

The filming was memorable for our producer, Tom Bronakoski. It was January of 1999, and the temperature on the ground was 1° Fahrenheit. Tom and his crew took off from Cutbank, Montana, in a Hiller 12E, a type of helicopter whose doors don't seal tightly, so you can imagine how cold it was in the air! Tom was impressed by the beauty of the Rocky Mountains rising in the distance and by the campsite's remoteness. His guide, a descendant of the Blackfoot tribe, told him that grizzly bears often come down from the mountains, following the Two Medicine River, which leads to the low valley where the Fight Tree still stands.

Our team reached the tree and gathered the seeds in the nick of time. When Helen West found the cottonwoods back in the sixties, at least three of them still stood. Now, due to time and the elements (and presumably a campfire that got out of control), only one of the cottonwoods and part of another remain. But their offspring are ready to fuel the imaginations of new generations.

Captain Lewis views the falls of the Missouri in this drawing by J. N. Marchand.

THE COTTONWOOD

When Lewis and Clark started their expedition, they knew that cottonwood trees (*Populus deltoides*) were good for making lightweight dugout canoes. More than once, that is how the expedition was able to continue to travel. According to their journals, they soon came to rely heavily on these native trees. For one thing, cottonwood trees have adapted to find water deep beneath the soil. Often, in an otherwise barren landscape, Lewis and Clark were relieved to find a wide-spreading cottonwood crown for shade and shelter from storms and as an indicator of water. Later they would find out from Indians that the bark of the cottonwood could serve as food for horses in harsh conditions.

As a matter of fact, one latter-day chronicler of their journey reported, "Of all the western trees, the cottonwood contributed more to the success of the Expedition than any other...Though we think it probable they would have successfully crossed the continent without the cottonwood, don't ask us how!"

Poplars, aspens, and cottonwoods are all members of the same genus. They're native to the Northern Hemisphere and are often the trees that first reforest a burned-out or barren area. The chubby, toothed leaves angle up in an almost triangular shape and usually have three to five large veins that meet near the stalk.

The wood of the common cottonwood is soft, used mostly for paper pulp, if anything. A full, shaggy, and comforting tree, the cottonwood feeds much wildlife, including grouse, deer, moose, beaver, hare, rabbit, porcupine, and bear. Today these trees still grow in clusters, happy reminders of the days when explorers roamed the plains and travel consisted of human and horse against nature—no helicopters to be seen.

Cottonwoods hold happy boyhood memories for me. Not far from our house, in Middle Amana, on the banks of Lily Lake, grew a great cottonwood tree. Here my friends and I had a tree house that was the site of many secret meetings. As a matter of fact, that tree was so large that when it was blown down by a tornado a few years ago, instead of removing it, someone cut a doorway in the trunk so that people could walk straight through it.

How to Grow a Cottonwood from Seed

JUNE: Gather the fruits from the cottonwood tree. Each fruit is a woody capsule, approximately a half inch to an inch long and somewhat pear-shaped. The capsules are green at first but should not be harvested until they turn light tan. Each capsule contains about thirty seeds, which are small, hard kernels surrounded by a hairy tuft similar to a dandelion. When the capsule is ripe, it opens and releases the seeds, which are dispersed as the hairy tufts float on the wind. It can be difficult to harvest the seeds because you must cut the capsules from the tree before they open. The best way to gauge when the capsules should be harvested is to pay attention to when the first few capsules split and release the cottony seeds. Fortunately, the capsules do not all split at the same time, so the collector will have time to gather the remaining intact capsules. Since the germination success rate for cottonwood seeds is usually high, you will likely need only two or three capsules for ten to twenty trees.

✿ Place the fruits in a dry paper bag in a warm location and let them dry completely. This should take only about one to three days. By this time the capsules should have split and spilled their seeds into the bag. If the capsule has not split on its own, gently cut it open and remove the seeds by hand.

☙ Plant the seeds immediately in a potting tray three to four inches deep filled with loose potting soil. Wet the soil completely, but let the tray drain until there is no more water coming out of the drainage holes. Place the seeds on the soil surface and put the entire tray in a large, clear plastic bag or cover tightly with clear plastic food wrap. Be sure to seal the end. The plastic should just rest on top of the planting tray but be taut enough not to rest on the soil surface. This forms a little greenhouse for the cottonwood seeds and protects them from extremes of temperature and moisture.

☙ Place the trays in an area protected from freezing, with lots of sunlight and temperatures from 72° to 85°F. Use a water-misting bottle to keep the soil just moist. Once the tiny sprouts begin to emerge, incorporate a liquid fertilizer at one-fifth strength for every other watering, and spray weekly with a fungicide to prevent mildew.

AUGUST: When the seedlings are two to three inches tall, carefully transplant each one to an individual three- or four-quart growing pot with potting soil. After five days, incorporate the liquid fertilizer at the recommended strength and fertilize once a week.

OCTOBER: When the seedlings reach a height of fifteen inches and the trunks are pencil-thick, plant them in the ground. The seedlings should be planted only if they have reached this approximate size and the weather is still mild. If they are still small and somewhat tender, keep them in the pots and place the pots outside until frost. This will trigger the seedlings to go dormant and drop their leaves. Then place the pots in an area where their soil won't freeze but where it will be cold enough to keep the seedlings dormant until spring. During this time it's important to maintain a low soil moisture level; keep the soil slightly damp but do not overwater. In the spring, put the seedlings outside to stimulate new leaf growth. For planting instructions, see page 118.

𝒲HERE TO 𝒫LANT 𝒴OUR 𝒞OTTONWOOD

A cottonwood probably isn't your best choice if you're a city dweller. However, if you want a tree that will grow large quickly and you have some space for it, the cottonwood fills the bill. Plant

GREAT PLAINS BEAUTY

The Great Plains don't have the lush beauty of eastern forests or the magnificent spectacles of the Pacific Northwest. To someone unfamiliar with the region, the sight of a lone, weathered cottonwood on the empty plains might not look too inviting. But to early settlers and Great Plains natives, such a sight was a treasure. The cottonwood is so beloved in the Plains states that it is one of the most popular symbols of the region, along with the bison and the western meadowlark.

it where there's sun, and at least fifty feet from the house, especially if it's a female. These trees do very well on creek banks and along ditches, providing wonderful shade and erosion control. Their heavy root systems hold soil in place and filter rain water, providing a healthier environment for fish and other wildlife. They are especially good for repopulating territory that's been decimated by fire, flood, or other natural disasters; if you plant a stand of cottonwoods, the landscape will be repopulated quickly. Also, they grow in such a way that the breeze will rustle the leaves, a lovely sound in a sparse landscape.

7
ANDREW JACKSON
SOUTHERN MAGNOLIA

A*BRAHAM LINCOLN* gets a lot of press for having been born in a log cabin, but the fact is President Andrew Jackson beat him to that distinction by a few decades. The third son of poor Irish immigrants, Jackson was born in South Carolina on March 15, 1767, a few days after the death of his father. His newly widowed mother was living with her sister's family. By all reports, Andrew's fiery temper fit in just fine with this animated clan; duels for honor were commonplace occurrences both at home and in the schoolyard.

When the Revolutionary War came to South Carolina, the Jackson boys were eager to join. Andrew's oldest brother, Hugh, died in battle early on; young Andrew and Robert were captured by a British raiding party in 1781. When fourteen-year-old Andrew refused to clean the boots of the British commander, citing his rights as a prisoner of war, the angry officer struck the boy with his sword, slashing Andrew's hand to the bone and wounding his head severely. Thus, with one slash of a sword, a political legend was born.

Unfortunately, both brothers caught smallpox as prisoners, and Robert died of it shortly after the boys were released and sent home. Their mother died of cholera a short time later. Thus it was Andrew who received a small inheritance from his grandfather in Ireland, and Andrew who lost it recklessly betting on cockfights and horse races.

Not unlike Patrick Henry, Andrew Jackson became a lawyer mostly because nothing else interested him. His military career as a general became the stuff of legend (his tough reputation led to the nickname "Old Hickory"). His winning of the Battle of New Orleans made him the most popular hero of the War of 1812. He

COMMON NAME: SOUTHERN MAGNOLIA

SCIENTIFIC NAME: *Magnolia grandiflora*

AKA: bull bay, evergreen magnolia, big-laurel, large-flower magnolia

STATE TREE: Mississippi

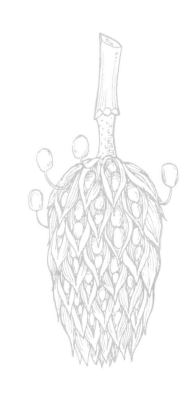

later served two very active terms as the seventh president of the United States.

Despite living the rough-and-tumble life of a military man, Jackson was known as a person of scrupulous morals and honor where women were concerned, and when he fell in love, he fell hard. Rachel Donelson was one of eleven children of Colonel John Donelson, who brought a party of 120 men, women, and children into the wilderness to found a town called Nashboro—later renamed Nashville, Tennessee. By all accounts, Rachel was beautiful; her face, figure, and personality made many men take notice. In 1785 the family moved to Kentucky; there Rachel married Lewis Robards, the son of a very wealthy Kentucky family. For three years they seemed happy—until Lewis caught Rachel in animated conversation with a young lawyer who was boarding at the Robards mansion. Lewis flew into a rage, and against the protestations of Rachel, the lawyer, and Lewis's own mother, he threw Rachel out of the house and warned her never to come back.

Back in seclusion at her mother's house, she caught the attention of another young lawyer, Andrew Jackson, who was boarding with her family. When her husband came to reunite with his wife, he accused Jackson of stealing her affections. His verbal attacks were so abusive he frequently had both Rachel and her mother in tears. Jackson angrily argued with and threatened Robards, who returned to his home; Rachel stayed with her mother.

Living in fear, Rachel felt she had to flee to Mississippi, and again Jackson offered to accompany her to safety. This time Lewis Robards publicly accused her of running off with Andrew Jackson, and he petitioned (and was granted) a right to divorce by the Virginia/Kentucky Congress.

Rachel's mother was beside herself. Not only had her daughter been rejected by Robards, the rather well-known Andrew Jackson's name was now being sullied as well; she was certain Jackson would be furious. Instead, on hearing Robards's slanders (by all accounts, Andrew had never even let there be an appearance of impropriety with Rachel), he offered to marry her. Her mother was profoundly grateful, reportedly asking, "You would sacrifice your life to save my child's good name?" to which he replied, "Ten thousand lives, Madam, if I had them."

By now, Andrew was totally smitten. He and Rachel were married in Natchez, Mississippi. Unfortunately, sometime later they discovered that what the legislature had granted Robards was permission to divorce; he hadn't actually gone through with the divorce. As soon as they found out, the divorce was completed and they remarried immediately.

HOME SWEET HOME

The southern magnolia is certainly one of this country's loveliest specimen trees, whether it's a solo front-yard show-stopper or planted in a stately row. But it's just plain home to the yellow-bellied sapsucker, red-cockaded woodpecker, and red-eyed vireo, who feed on its red berries, as do squirrels, opossums, quail, and turkey.

Andrew Jackson's positions became ever more prominent; he oversaw the not always smooth transition as Florida was bought from Spain. He and Rachel settled happily outside of Nashville at their estate, the Hermitage. Jackson relished public life; Rachel preferred a much quieter existence and often stayed in her room with her Bible. But by all accounts the marriage was happy. Rachel loved the Hermitage and enjoyed the beautiful nature that surrounded her. Jackson went on to become a congressman and a senator in Washington; it wasn't until 1828, when he ran for president, that life went awry for the Jacksons.

If you think campaigning can be a nasty business today, you wouldn't believe what went on back then. The attacks on Jackson were unrelenting and almost completely fabricated. His marriage to Rachel proved to be his Achilles' heel, and the opposition was tireless in the assassination of her character. She was portrayed as an adulteress at best, a seductress or loose woman more often. Andrew did his best to try to shield her from these attacks, but she was very deeply stricken by what was said.

When news came that he had won the presidency, his comment was, "I am filled with gratitude. Still, my mind is depressed." His state of mind was justified. On December 22, during the short weeks between the election and Jackson's inauguration, his beloved Rachel died of a sudden heart attack. He was certain—as was most everyone—that this was caused by the accusations against her.

He never got over her death, and he never remarried. He took to Washington a descendant of one of Rachel's favorite magnolia trees from the garden at the Hermitage and planted it at the White House in memory of his beloved.

THE WHITE HOUSE MAGNOLIA

If you have an old twenty-dollar bill, take it out and look at it. On the back you'll find an engraving of the White House, and to

The Andrew Jackson southern magnolia (*Magnolia grandiflora*) on the White House lawn.

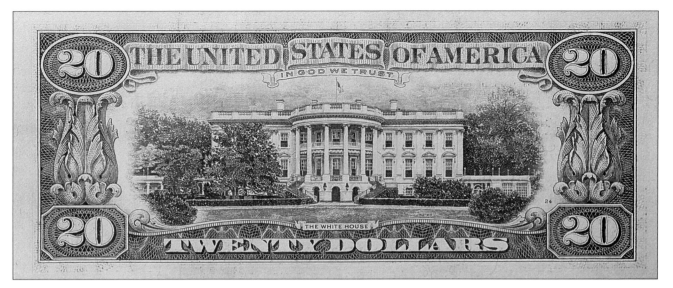

You may have a historic tree in your pocket. The Andrew Jackson Southern Magnolia, planted in 1828, is to the left of the rear portico of the White House.

one side is the magnolia that Andrew Jackson planted. I've been fortunate to have visited the White House several times, and without a doubt this magnolia is my favorite tree there. It was also the favorite of Lady Bird Johnson—a tireless advocate of trees and wildflowers—so much so that she took descendants of it back to Texas to plant at Goliad and LBJ's boyhood home.

Rachel's magnolia is distinguished in another way: several years ago, when a disturbed person attempted to fly a small airplane into the White House living quarters, it hit the magnolia and crashed without doing much damage to the White House itself. A large limb on the magnolia was lost, but the tree may have kept the First Family from harm, as Andrew no doubt wished he could have shielded Rachel.

It's always a special thrill for me to become acquainted with the descendants of the original planters of these trees, and, needless to say, I was delighted to become friends with Andrew Jackson VI. (Ever since Andrew and Rachel, who did not have children of their own, adopted her nephew, named Andrew Jackson, Jr., it's been family tradition to name the eldest boy Andrew and the eldest girl Rachel.) Andrew also lives and works in Tennessee as a lawyer. He has a great spirit and a great story to tell.

In 1998 a terrible tornado tore through parts of Tennessee, including the Hermitage, and many trees were uprooted, some of which had been planted or commissioned by Andrew Jackson himself. The grounds of the Hermitage were ravaged. This sad situ-

The southern magnolia is native to the Deep South, from the southern coast of North Carolina down to the swamps of Louisiana, where it enjoys a truly sublime existence. But Yankees who want to import a bit of southern glory are having some luck growing magnolias as far north as the southern-most parts of the northeastern states and the most temperate spots in the Northwest. Except for the hybrids developed expressly for their cold-hardiness, chances are a magnolia grown outside of its native region won't grow as tall or as broad as it does in the South, and its flowers won't be nearly as lush or abundant as its southern counterparts.

ation led to my first meeting with Andrew V and Andrew VI; we made arrangements to replant descendants of the White House Magnolia, which was, of course, an offspring of the Andrew Jackson Magnolia. The tree had come full circle.

THE SOUTHERN MAGNOLIA

Like Rachel Jackson herself, the southern magnolia (*Magnolia grandiflora*) can be considered a beauty that needs special care in order to flourish. This is a magnificent tree—sixty to one hundred feet tall, with a spread of thirty to fifty feet. In other words, consider the size of your landscape before planting the tree. It will certainly become a focus of attention. But if it is correctly planted in the right location—what a treat! The leaves are dark green and shiny, often with a hairy underside. The blossoms, which appear from late spring to midsummer, are a full six to nine inches wide, in a cup shape with many white petals (from six to sixteen). The fragrance of the flowers is unparalleled.

Some of the most beautiful wood carvings I have ever seen were made from magnolia wood.

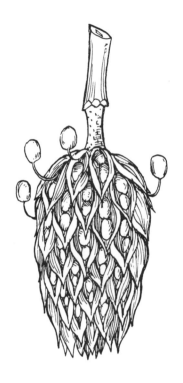

SEPTEMBER: Gather the fruits from the magnolia tree. The fruits are rusty brown, cone-shaped, and appear at the end of the branches after the flowers have fallen. Within the fuzz-covered fruit are many half-inch-long red-fleshed seeds. The removable outer portion of the seed is soft and easily scraped off, while the portion you will plant is hard, almost stony. To grow ten to twenty trees, you will need only two or three fruits, which bear between ten and twenty seeds. Do not harvest the fruits until the red seed coat is visible.

❧ Once the fruits have been harvested, they should be laid out on a flat, dry surface in sunlight until they crack open to allow easy removal of the seeds. Discard the empty cone and prepare to scrape away the fleshy seed coat. The easiest way to do this is to soak the seeds in water overnight and scrape the seed coat off by hand. Then place the dry, defleshed seeds in a large, resealable plastic bag. In a large bowl, mix three cups of coarse-grade perlite with three cups of water so that it is thoroughly moist. With a slotted spoon, add the drained perlite to the seeds in the bag and lightly toss to thoroughly mix. Mark the date on the bag, seal it tight, and put it in the vegetable storage bin of the refrigerator at a temperature of 40° to 44°F. The seeds need to remain in the refrigerator for ninety days.

❧ Check the seeds every second week, looking for mold. If mold appears, rinse the seeds in a ten-to-one solution of water and household bleach, mix with a new batch of moist perlite, and re-seal in a new plastic bag, dated with the original date.

FEBRUARY: By this time the seeds should have been refrigerated for ninety days, and it is time to transfer them to planting trays three to four inches deep filled with loose potting soil. Remove the seeds from the perlite and place them on the soil surface in rows two to three inches apart, then cover with a quarter inch of soil.

❧ Place the trays in an area protected from freezing, with lots of sunlight and temperatures from 72° to 85°F. Use a water-misting bottle to keep the soil just moist. Once the tiny sprouts begin to emerge, incorporate a liquid fertilizer at one-fifth strength for every other watering, and spray weekly with a fungicide to prevent mildew.

MAY: When the seedlings are two to three inches tall, carefully transplant each one to an individual three- or four-quart growing pot with potting soil. After five days, incorporate the liquid fertilizer at the recommended strength and fertilize once a week.

AUGUST: When the seedlings reach a height of fifteen inches and the trunks are pencil-thick, plant them in the ground. If they have not reached this height, leave them in the growing pots over the winter. For planting instructions, see page 118.

WHERE TO PLANT YOUR SOUTHERN MAGNOLIA

The southern magnolia thrives in the warmer states in full sun and in soil that gets plenty of water but not too much. It also needs a lot of magnesium; I usually add Osnocote fertilizer, which you can buy at any garden store, to the planting hole. The roots are slow to take hold, and the tree can use some coddling. The young wood is soft; the tree will do best if you allow the lower branches to remain, not removing them until the tree is older.

8
JOHNNY APPLESEED
RAMBO APPLE TREE

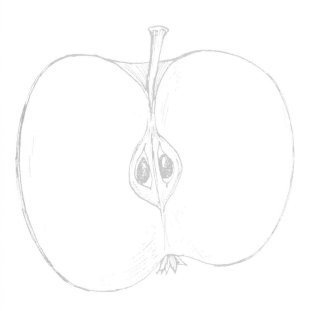

COMMON NAME: RAMBO APPLE
SCIENTIFIC NAME: *Pyrus malus*

IT'S HARD for those of us who live in modern times and have a huge selection of foods available year-round to understand the historical importance of apples. To settlers in the nineteenth century, the thing that marked the difference between successfully staking a claim and losing your land was the availability of subsistence foods. In fact, parts of both the Kentucky and Ohio territories made it a requirement that homesteaders plant apple or peach orchards, a sign that the land was being cultivated.

Apple trees are one of the few trees that will bear usable fruit within five years of being planted as seedlings—a godsend for the settlers. Apples were counted on year-round. During the summer months, the fruit was eaten straight from the tree; leftover sweet apples were buried in pits to keep them fresh until well after the first frost. Apples were made into vinegar for cooking and cider for preserving. Apple butter was a staple (and one of the few foods that would last as a preserve all winter). Many barrels of apple cider were used as a nutritious beverage throughout the year, and hard cider was often used as currency to trade for other crops, chickens, or tools. Apple brandy from up North brought a good price in New Orleans.

But there were no apple orchards on the western frontier and no place for the settlers to go to obtain seeds. This is where Johnny Appleseed's genius came in. He got many bushels of seeds free as leftovers from the cider mills of western Pennsylvania. Then he headed for the frontier, to places where there were either a few settlers or it seemed likely there would be within a few years. He'd pick a flat, sunny piece of land and sow an orchard. By the time homesteaders arrived, he had an orchard waiting for them, complete with apples—and, more important, seeds—for purchase.

There were other nurserymen on the frontier, but Johnny's importance lies in the fact that he was itinerant—always on the move, buying many tracts of land and sowing orchard after orchard.

JOHNNY APPLESEED

If you ask most Americans about Johnny Appleseed, they'll think of a strange-looking folk hero with a pot on his head who planted apple seeds. Was he man? Myth? Or just a good story for schoolchildren?

In fact, Johnny Appleseed was an educated man by the name of John Chapman. While he was very much a man of his times, his progressive thinking combined with practical action make him a wonderful role model for the modern world.

John Chapman was born in Leominster, Massachusetts, the second son of a carpenter/farmer. His mother died when he was two, and shortly thereafter his father left home to fight in the Revolutionary War. John's father lost his farms during the war but managed to start over afterward. His new life included a new wife, with whom he had ten more children.

By all accounts, John was a boy with two passions—his faith (he always carried a well-worn New Testament in the pocket of his overalls) and nature. As a teenager he became a follower of the ideas of Swedish theologian Emanuel Swedenborg, whose ideas of mysticism and God's presence in all nature fit well with John's own leanings.

After schooling and two years as a missionary, John returned to his father's farm. There was much excitement in Massachusetts about the cheap land to be had on the western frontier—which at that point was Pennsylvania, western New York, and Ohio. Almost all of the young men talked about it, but two—John and his half-brother Nathaniel—packed up and headed for their uncle's claim outside a tiny settlement called Pittsburgh.

The story goes that on the frontier, John was accidentally kicked in the head by his mule and fell into a coma. He awoke several days later to report his near-death experience: he'd seen the beauties of heaven but had been told by an angel that it was not yet his time to die. A couple of days later, he had a second vision of heaven. This time he saw clearly that the streets of heaven were lined with fruit trees. Afterward he said to his brother, "Now I know my life's work; I am going to sow the West with apple seeds, making the wilderness to blossom with their beauty and people

Johnny Appleseed on a postage stamp.

As we walked through the apple orchard, grown up in tall bluegrass, Ántonia kept stopping to tell me about one tree or another. "I love them as if they were people," she said, rubbing her hand over the bark.

❧

WILLA CATHER,
MY ÁNTONIA

happy with their fruit." Whether that is exactly what happened or not, he embraced this mission until his death.

THE RAMBO APPLE

Those of us who shop for apples at the supermarket today might suppose that there are only six to a dozen types from which to choose. In fact, there are over a thousand varieties of apples. In Johnny's day, orchards were much more prevalent and ordinary folks fancied themselves connoisseurs, discussing the merits of various apples much as wine connoisseurs discuss grapes and vintages today. Everyone had several favorites, because different apples fulfilled particular culinary needs: there were baking apples, sauce apples, drying apples, cider apples, and dessert apples. Thomas Jefferson fancied Esopus Spitzenbergs; Ben Franklin was so enamored of Newton Pippins that he had barrels of them shipped to England when he was there on behalf of the colonies.

Richard Algeo and a granddaughter with the last living Johnny Appleseed Rambo Apple.

The familiar varieties usually found on today's supermarket shelves, alas, have not been chosen for taste or quality; they have become the godfathers of apples because they can be grown perfectly round, they keep their color even when turning to mush, and, most important, they ship well.

But there are the makings of an apple renaissance these days. In Europe, where people eat far more apples than Americans do, tasty new varieties are gaining a popular foothold. Even in this country, adventurous eaters are becoming more willing to try a slightly lopsided fruit that is recommended by a grower in the know. (Author and apple aficionado Roger Yepsen suggests stopping at orchard fruit stands and asking the growers which fruits they recommend as a way of adding color to your apple palette.)

One of John Chapman's favorite apples was a dessert apple called the Rambo. (Most of the apples we purchase today are dessert apples, which just means they're sweet enough to eat by themselves without some sort of preparation.) One of America's oldest varieties, Chapman's favorite was named for Peter Gunnarson Rambo, an early colonist. Rambo took Swedish seeds with him in 1640 to the New Sweden colony, which briefly encompassed Delaware, southeastern Pennsylvania, and southern New Jersey. By the time it became one of Chapman's favorites, the Rambo was popular as both a cider and a dessert apple.

The Rambo is yellowish green if it is picked tart in July for pie making. If it is allowed to ripen on the tree until August or early September, reddish stripes will appear on the sunny side of the flesh. The Rambo is particularly crisp and juicy and is sometimes called a "bread and cheese" apple—a rather more specific denotation of its dessert status. The hardy, vigorous tree can reach a height of thirty-five to forty feet if planted with plenty of root space.

Cherie Lucks, great-great-grand-niece of John Chapman.

THE ALGEOS' TREE

In 1994 I was thrilled to find that still standing on a 160-year-old Ohio farm was a living apple tree that had been documented as having been planted by Johnny himself. Not only had the local historical society authenticated the tree, the Algeo family itself had passed down stories of Johnny's visits, when he'd sleep in the small cabin beside the house. Their great old tree had supplied many generations with apples, but by the time we heard of it, it had decayed inside and was barely producing fruit. Still, with the enthusiastic help of the Algeo family, we were able to take both softwood and root cuttings from the tree before it became badly damaged by a storm. Dale Bryan of the Hollydale Nursery in Tennessee helped us use a form of grafting called T budding, in which the cuttings from Johnny's Ohio tree were

The cabin at the Algeos' farm where Johnny Appleseed slept.

budded into envelopes of bark on other apple-tree rootstocks.

Johnny Appleseed's last known tree has now provided us with 10,000 seedling trees ready for planting, to continue his heritage in yards and orchards across the United States.

GRAFTING

There is a note of irony here. Johnny himself never liked the idea of grafting, which was common practice in his day. Grafting is even more widespread today because apple trees are peculiar. You can take seeds from the sweetest apples, and the new tree may bear sour fruit. There is just no way to be certain that a tree grown from seed will bear the variety and quality of apples that you want. When you graft, however, you take a part of a living tree and make it part of another tree, then eventually cut off all the branches that had previously grown above the graft. Because you're growing a continuation of the parent tree, you will have exactly the same apples.

Grafting isn't easy for the layman to do; it requires careful instruction and steady hands or a couple hundred dollars' worth of tools. If you're curious about grafting, I'd suggest you read a thorough book on the subject, such as *Know It and Grow It* by Carl Whitcomb.

John Chapman objected to grafting on a theological basis, saying, "They can improve the apple in that way, but that is only a device of man, and it is wicked to cut up trees that way. The correct method is to select good seeds and plant them in good ground and God only can improve the apples."

To tell you the truth, I myself favor grafting only when there's no other choice—as was the case with Johnny's last apple tree. I think it is wonderful and miraculous to grow trees from seeds: like snowflakes, each is programmed to be slightly different; each will be unique.

HOW TO GROW AN APPLE TREE FROM SEED

SEPTEMBER: Pick thirty desirable apples from trees. Don't be tempted to gather "drops"—apples that have already fallen to the ground—as they tend to have larvae or fungus invasions when they have been on the ground for more than twenty-four hours. And store-bought apples are often infertile from being kept in cold storage over time, so just go for the tree-picked real thing.

GREAT-GREAT-GREAT-GRANDMA ALGEO'S APPLESAUCE COOKIES

³/₄ CUP SOFT SHORTENING

1 CUP BROWN SUGAR, PACKED

1 EGG

¹/₂ CUP APPLESAUCE

2¹/₄ CUP ALL-PURPOSE FLOUR, SIFTED

¹/₂ TEASPOON BAKING SODA

¹/₂ TEASPOON SALT

³/₄ TEASPOON CINNAMON

¹/₄ TEASPOON GROUND CLOVES

1 CUP SEEDLESS RAISINS

¹/₂ CUP CHOPPED WALNUTS

Mix the shortening, sugar, and egg thoroughly. Stir in the applesauce. Combine the dry ingredients and blend into the shortening/sugar/egg mixture. Mix in the raisins and nuts. Drop spoonfuls of the batter onto a greased baking sheet. Bake at 375° for 10 to 12 minutes. The recipe makes 4 dozen cookies.

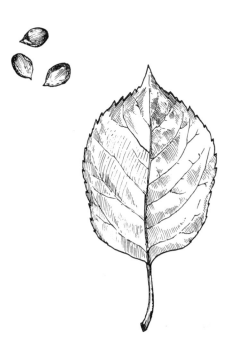

🐝 Carefully remove the seeds from the apple cores. Gently wash off all the pulp from the seeds with room-temperature water, being careful not to break or pierce the seeds. Rinse the seeds thoroughly three times.

🐝 Place the seeds in a large, resealable plastic bag. In a large bowl, mix three cups of coarse-grade perlite with three cups of water so that it is completely moist. With a slotted spoon, add the drained perlite to the seeds in the bag and lightly toss to thoroughly mix. Mark the date on the bag, seal it, and put it in the vegetable storage bin of the refrigerator at a temperature of 40° to 44°F. The seeds will need to remain in the refrigerator for thirty to sixty days.

🐝 Check the seeds every second week, looking for mold. If mold appears, rinse the seeds in a ten-to-one solution of water and household bleach, mix them with a new batch of moist perlite, and reseal in a new plastic bag, dated with the original date.

MARCH: Prepare planting trays three to four inches deep filled with loose potting soil. Remove the seeds from the perlite and place them on the soil surface in rows two to three inches apart, then cover with a half inch of soil. A thin layer of sawdust or wood shavings applied over the soil surface encourages seed emergence and discourages mildew.

🐝 Place the trays in an area protected from freezing, with lots of sunlight and temperatures from 72° to 85°F. Use a water-misting bottle twice a day to keep the soil just moist. Once the tiny sprouts begin to emerge, incorporate a liquid fertilizer at one-fifth strength for every other watering, and spray weekly with a fungicide to prevent mildew.

MAY: When the seedlings are two to three inches tall, carefully transplant each one to an individual three- or four-quart growing pot with potting soil. After three days, incorporate liquid houseplant fertilizer at the recommended strength and fertilize at every other watering.

AUGUST: When the seedlings reach a height of fifteen inches and the trunks are pencil-thick, plant them in the ground. For planting instructions, see page 118.

WHERE TO PLANT YOUR APPLE TREE

Choosing a good spot for planting is half the battle. Planting a tree on a high spot rather than in a hollow or at the bottom of a hill will help avoid damage from late frosts. (Frosts tend to "settle," not rise.)

Give the tree some space. Good air circulation is important and will ward off problems such as powdery mildew. (If mildew ever becomes a problem, a couple of steps can be taken: first, use a sulfur-based fungicide before bearing season, then continue the sulfur treatments from blossom time until the fruit forms.)

CARING FOR YOUR APPLE TREE

Pruning is essential. Take off any diseased branches and thin out branches that are tending toward crowding. The tree canopy needs to be open to sunlight and air circulation. Each tree has slightly different pruning requirements, taking into consideration not only the variety but the situation in which it's planted. There are several very good books that will get you started pruning your specific tree; an excellent introduction to the subject is P. P. Pirone's *Tree Maintenance.*

(Above) Jeff Meyer pruning the first Rambo Apple descendants.

(Right) The historical plaque outside the Algeos' Ohio farm.

9
Mark Twain Cave Bur Oak

CO YOU REMEMBER a book that thrilled you or kept you awake reading long into the night when you were a kid? Long before Harry Potter arrived on the scene, Mark Twain entranced readers with the hair-raising adventures and outrageous antics of Tom Sawyer and Huck Finn. I loved those books when I was growing up, and I especially loved the parts that scared me to death. And nothing was scarier than the time Tom and Becky got lost in the darkness of a huge cave and Tom made a terrifying discovery there. Mark Twain's descriptions of the cave are so detailed, so real, that each reader surely imagines himself or herself hopelessly lost in the damp darkness along with Becky and Tom.

When I was older, I learned that Mark Twain was the pen name of humorist Samuel Clemens, who had grown up in Hannibal, Missouri, not all that far from the Iowa of my boyhood. Young Sam moved there in 1839 at the age of four and lived there until he was seventeen. As anyone who has visited Hannibal knows, Clemens based many of his fictional locales and characters on local places and folks—including the famous cave. The limestone geology of the area, with its many bluffs, makes caves quite common.

During the winter of 1820, a man named Jack Simms was out hunting with his dog when the dog took off after a small animal. Within minutes, both the animal and the dog disappeared, seemingly into a sheer cliff wall. The canine soon reappeared next to a big bur oak tree in a small opening into a very large, very deep cave. Simms Cave, as it soon came to be known, was unusual for Missouri. Instead of having several large caverns, it is what's called a "maze cave," because the interior consists of long, narrow, interconnecting passages where limestone formations join each other. The passages in this cave total two miles, and at one point five

COMMON NAME: BUR OAK
SCIENTIFIC NAME: *Quercus macrocarpa*
AKA: mossy-cup oak, prairie oak

pathways converge: the perfect place for intrigue, both real and fictional.

Simms Cave soon became a place of fascination, attracting all kinds of attention. It took on even greater mystique in the 1840s, when a local doctor named Joseph Nash McDowell purchased the cave, put a heavy wooden door on it, and locked it securely. Whispered conjecture probably didn't even come close to the strange reality of what went on inside. It turned out that McDowell, a gifted surgeon, was also intrigued by research on cadavers. When his fourteen-year-old daughter died, the bereaved father wanted to mummify and preserve her remains, and to that end he suspended her body in an oversized copper-and-glass flask inside the cave. Once the truth of what lay behind the door was discovered, you'd better believe word shot through sleepy Hannibal like a cannonball. Despite the maelstrom of local outrage, the girl's body remained in the cave for another year before it was removed for a more traditional burial.

All of this intrigue made the cave, and the large bur oak outside of it, a magnet for the local children, young Sam Clemens chief among them. In his autobiography, Clemens recounts how much he enjoyed consorting with the cave's only remaining residents—the bats.

Mark Twain at the Mississippi River.

> I know all about these Chiroptera [bats], because our great cave, three miles below Hannibal, was multitudinously stocked with them, and often I brought them home to amuse my mother with. It was easy to manage if it was a school day, because then I had ostensibly been to school and hadn't any bats. She was not a suspicious person, but full of trust and confidence; and when I said, "There's something in my pocket for you," she would put her hand in. But she always took it out again, herself; I didn't have to tell her. It was remarkable, the way she couldn't learn to like private bats.
>
> I think she was never in the cave in her life; but everybody else went up there . . . It was an easy place to get lost in; anybody could do it—including the bats. I got lost in it myself, along with a lady, and our last candle burned down to almost nothing before we glimpsed the search party's lights winding about in the distance.

Clemens's own experience set the stage for the harrowing adventure of Tom Sawyer and Becky Thatcher.

Almost as well known to local youths as the cave is the bur oak that guards its entrance—surely the one Sam Clemens and his friends climbed and lounged in, perhaps smoking a corncob pipe,

The Mark Twain Bur Oak (*Quercus macrocarpa*) near the cave in Hannibal, Missouri, where Samuel Clemens played as a boy.

searching the sky, spinning their own yarns on an indolent summer afternoon.

That tree still stands today, its roots running deep into the Missouri soil, much as Sam's Missouri roots ran deep in his private and professional life. Simms Cave is known now as the Mark Twain Cave; hence the Mark Twain Cave Bur Oak. The Missouri Department of Conservation has dated the tree back to 1731, so it was already a grand landmark during the days Sam played hooky and headed for the cave.

For me, the Mark Twain Cave Bur Oak stands as a testimony to American childhood—the adventure, moral dilemmas, fun, and mischief experienced by each of us back during those days when our moms learned to be careful before putting their hands into our jeans or coat pockets.

THE BUR OAK

The bur (or mossy-cup) oak (*Quercus macrocarpa*) has always seemed like a friendly tree to me; the spread of its sheltering branches often rivals its height. It has a broad, round top and the lower limbs often droop, so it's perfect for climbing or building tree forts. I have very dramatic memories of bur oaks in the Iowa landscape, especially in the wintertime. It seemed one would rise up suddenly in a hedgerow or on an incline, its totally black trunk

posing against the white snow. I have special memories of these trees in summer also. I remember sauntering toward a lone bur oak planted as a landmark in the middle of a cornfield or seeing the cattle clustered under one that provided shade and relief from the heat.

One of my favorite trees in the world is a bur oak that grows on the campus of Vanderbilt University, where I went to school. A historic beauty, predating the college by several hundred years (bur oaks can live to be five hundred or six hundred years old), it still stands outside the campus dining hall. Many times, weather permitting, I'd grab my college "health" food (usually hamburgers) and sit beneath it, sharing my bounty with the squirrels.

I remember the sculpted leaves unfurling as a sure sign of spring; the full, proud coat of green worn throughout the summer; and the quick blaze of orange and yellows that announced the end of fall. But I loved that tree most when it was barren of leaves. For then I could lie on the ground and look straight up, seeing how high those mighty branches pierced the sky.

Bur oaks preceded the pioneers as they headed west; groves of bur oaks were often chosen as great potential home sites. The wood is flexible and waterproof, making it ideal for barrels and boats; however, the sheer number of branches that have to be removed from the trunk makes it less than popular among loggers.

Bur oaks are easily recognized by their large acorns—a four-course meal for any lucky squirrel. The seed itself looks as though it's protruding from a mossy cup or an Easter basket, a woven half-circle topped with straw. Trees don't produce acorns for seven or eight years; once they get started, they can produce as many as 5,000 a year! They provide a favorite feast—rich in carbohydrates and fats (not unlike our dessert!)—for scores of birds, forest animals, and insects. By the time the seeds are divvied up, only thirty or forty may remain to sprout in the wild. Perhaps half of these will reach maturity.

The bur oak's leaves have at least one deep set of indentations, dividing it into at least two and often three or four portions.

How to Grow a Bur Oak from Seed

OCTOBER: Gather the oak tree's fruits, which are the acorns. They are one and a half to two inches long, oblong to oval, green at first, turning tan-brown as they ripen, and topped with a corky overcap that is scaly in appearance. Acorns can be gathered from the tree, but they must be fully ripe, showing no green. Or you can collect them from the ground, avoiding those with tiny weevil holes and those that feel hollow. Each fruit contains one seed, so for ten to twenty trees, gather twenty to forty acorns. If you float the acorns in a bucket of water, the best ones will sink; discard those that float.

❧ Place the acorns in an open container and allow them to dry completely, which should take only a few days. Then remove the scaly overcap and keep only the acorn. (Be careful not to puncture the seed coat during this process.) If the scaly overcap is difficult to remove, let it remain attached to the acorn and within two or three days it should be ready to plant.

❧ Plant the acorns immediately in planting trays three to four inches deep filled with loose potting soil. Place them in rows two to three inches apart, then cover them with a quarter inch of soil.

❧ Place the trays in an area protected from freezing, with lots of sunlight and temperatures from 72° to 85°F. Use a water-misting bottle to keep the soil just moist. Once the tiny sprouts begin to emerge, incorporate a liquid fertilizer at one-quarter strength for every other watering, and spray weekly with a fungicide.

JANUARY: When the seedlings are two to three inches tall, carefully transplant them to individual three- or four-quart growing pots with potting soil. After five days, incorporate the liquid fertilizer at the recommended strength and fertilize once a week.

MAY: When the seedlings reach a height of fifteen inches and the trunks are pencil-thick, plant them in the ground. For planting instructions, see page 118.

Where to Plant Your Bur Oak

What sort of spot is best? Well, a bur oak needs lots of room, both height and width. Don't plant it too close to the house or directly under telephone wires. And if you're planting it in a yard with grass, be sure to give it a wide base of mulch, for its early root system occupies the same stratum underground as the grass does—and turf will always win the water wars. Within a decade, the tree should be an impressive twenty feet high, shooting for a final size of fifty to eighty feet and a canopy spread, side to side, of forty to one hundred feet.

Oak Lore

Of all trees, oaks may be surrounded by the richest body of myth and symbolism. The oak appears in the Bible, ancient Greek and Roman legends, and even druidic lore. The tree figures in several lively episodes in the story of Zeus and company as well as in the story of Christ and the crucifixion. When Cain murdered Abel, the Bible says that Cain had to carry his brother's body for seven hundred years and then bury him. To mark the burial place, Cain stuck his staff in the ground, and seven oaks immediately sprang forth in a row, in a place now known as the Seven Oaks of Palestine. One favorite oak legend puts the stork in its place: in Germany, babies are said to come from oak trees and are brought from the tree to the family by a doctor.

10
WALDEN WOODS
RED MAPLE

COMMON NAME: RED MAPLE

SCIENTIFIC NAME: *Acer rubrum*

AKA: swamp maple, scarlet maple, soft maple

STATE TREE: Rhode Island

*T*O THE GOOD FOLKS of Concord, Massachusetts, in the mid-1800s, Henry David Thoreau wasn't exactly a revered celebrity. He was a local fellow who couldn't cut it as a teacher, thought of himself as a writer, occasionally ran his dad's pencil factory, and spent a couple of years living by himself at a nearby pond, writing a book about it that was a modest success. At least the publisher didn't dump all of the unsold copies of *Walden* on his doorstep, as they did with the 700 remainders of his *A Week on the Concord and Merrimack Rivers.*

Henry himself knew that to all outward appearances, his life looked like a failure. "If a man walks in the woods for love of them half of each day, he is in danger of being regarded as a loafer; but if he spends his whole day as a speculator, shearing off those woods and making the earth bald before her time, he is esteemed as an industrious and enterprising citizen," he wrote. In many ways a man before his time, Thoreau did not buy into his neighbors' definition of success. Most men, he observed, "live lives of quiet desperation." Their continual chasing of the dollar to furnish unnecessarily large houses with pretentious furniture and to dress according to the empty dictates of fashion rendered them slaves. "There are so many subtle masters that enslave both North and South. It is hard to have a Southern overseer; it is worse to have a Northern one; but worst of all is when you are the slave-driver of yourself." Opinions like these might have made him an icon of generations yet to come, but they did not make him very popular with his neighbors.

Henry David Thoreau was the bright son of working-class parents. He so impressed his schoolmasters as a young student that he ended up going to Harvard—although once there, he refused to "play the game." He used the classes and library for his own ends and graduated in the middle of his class.

He returned to Concord to become a schoolmaster himself, but he didn't have the heart for discipline or teaching by rote, and he quit after only two weeks. He and his brother, John, soon opened a progressive school and made a successful go of it for three years until John took ill. In 1839 Henry and John took a canoe trip along the Concord and Merrimack rivers that changed Henry's life. Somehow on that trip nature spoke to him in such a profound way that he decided his calling was not as a schoolmaster but as a poet of nature.

Fortunately for Thoreau, during his schooldays at Harvard, Ralph Waldo Emerson, a leading poet, writer, lecturer, and leader of the transcendentalist movement, had settled in Concord. In him Henry found a mentor, father figure, and friend. Many of Thoreau's first writings were published in *The Dial,* a magazine with which Emerson had close ties, and Thoreau's ideas about spirituality and nature found a resounding echo in transcendentalism, which celebrated the individual rather than the masses, emotion rather than reason, and nature rather than man.

"*Too Fair to be Believed*"

Thoreau's cabin in Walden Woods.

In 1836, Henry spent six weeks living with a friend at his rustic lakeside cabin. We have no record of what happened there, but apparently it was such a positive experience that when Emerson gave Thoreau permission to stay at a pond on a piece of property outside of town, Thoreau leaped at the chance. He set about building himself a small cabin on Walden Pond and moved out there on Independence Day in 1845 to write, reflect, and meditate. He stayed for two years. In the second chapter of *Walden: or, Life in the Woods*, he explained, "I went to the woods because I wished to live deliberately, to front only the essential facts of life, and see if I could not learn what it had to teach, and not, when I came to die, discover that I had not lived."

To Thoreau, Walden Pond was "the earth's eye," the trees along the shore "the slender eyelashes which fringe it, and the wooded hills and cliffs around it are its overhanging brows." Of all his wonderful enchantment with the nature of the place, one thing that held the greatest enchantment for him was the red maple tree. Time and time again, he pondered and wrote of the glory of these trees, especially as their leaves turned in autumn.

How beautiful, when a whole [red maple] tree is like one great scarlet fruit full of ripe juices, every leaf, from lowest limb to topmost spire, all aglow, especially if you look toward the sun! What more remarkable object can there be in the landscape? Visible for miles, too fair to be believed. If such a phenomenon occurred but once, it would be handed down by tradition to posterity, and get into the mythology at last.

To my mind, three important things happened at Walden Pond. Thoreau came to a profound understanding of himself and nature, he wrote a classic book, and he became one of America's first conservationists. As hard as it may be to believe, the splendors of nature have not always been viewed with awe. Seventeenth-century Puritans such as William Bradford found the unspoiled terrain of America to be "a hideous and desolate wilderness full of wild beasts and wild men." Bradford felt the wilderness symbolized the evil just beyond godly civilization, and as such it led men to their lowest natures and tempted them to sin.

While many of our founding fathers had a great appreciation of nature, most of Thoreau's contemporaries assumed its resources were never-ending and existed for the use and convenience of humankind. Thoreau, on the other hand, was alarmed at the steady disappearance of woods and meadows. "I feel that each town should have a park, or rather a primitive forest . . . where a stick should never be cut for fuel, nor for the Navy, nor to make

HENRY DAVID THOREAU

wagons, but stand and decay for higher uses—a common possession forever, for instruction and recreation . . . We are all schoolmasters and our schoolhouse is the Universe."

He was also alarmed that encroachments were already being made on the acreage surrounding Walden Pond. He believed in the interdependency of all living things; to cut down the forests and force many species from their homes was to do irreparable harm. "What is the use of a house if you haven't got a tolerable planet to put it on?"

Walden is now regarded as a masterpiece and savored by people from many different countries. Each time I've visited Walden Woods, I've met people from all over the world, each of whom had a spirit of awe. They were seeing the nature surrounding them with new eyes—with Thoreau's eyes—and magic was reborn in every twig and leaf.

Heywood's Meadow in the snow at Walden Woods.

*F*IGHTING THE *G*OOD *F*IGHT

I first became involved with Walden Woods in 1990, during a crisis that Thoreau himself would have understood. A developer had purchased the land around Walden Pond with the idea of building condos. Many folks who had read and been inspired by *Walden*— and even many who hadn't—felt that this land was special. If any place should be preserved for posterity, this was at the top of their list. A group of supporters rallied to raise money to buy the property back and make it a preserve for future generations. One of the main proponents of the Walden Woods Project was the musician Don Henley. Don is a nice guy and very interested in conservation. Over the years, whenever he and I were together, we enjoyed discussing tree planting and preservation, which he is involved with in locations throughout the United States. Another benefit of my involvement with the Walden Woods Project was that I met Executive Director Kathi Anderson, who became one of my close friends. We share a great interest in trees and preservation and, of

Don Henley at
Walden Pond.

course, an appreciation of Walden Woods. Thanks to the efforts of great folks like Don and Kathi, the land is now permanently protected, and there is an ongoing effort to create the Thoreau Institute and to restore historic structures on the property.

We decided to grow the offspring of a Walden Woods tree not only to generate funds but to heighten awareness of the project; nothing seemed more fitting as a symbol of Walden than one of Thoreau's beloved red maples. I can see why he especially loved this tree. It is beautiful and distinctive in every season, from the first flowering buds of spring to the scarlet and blazing yellow of autumn, whether it is wearing a finery of green or is blanketed in a gentle snow. Thoreau was right: if one tree had only once made such magnificent changes, it would have become a thing of myth.

The Red Maple

The red maple (*Acer rubrum*) is very easy to grow and therefore makes a great starter tree for someone new to tree planting. It is often used for landscaping and decoration, since it is one of the very first trees to blossom in spring, and in the autumn, as Thoreau says, the flaming red leaves are "too fair to be believed." The red maple is a medium or large tree, usually forty to seventy feet in height (although occasionally one will grow as tall as one hundred feet!), with a trunk diameter of two to four feet. If planted in the open, it has a rather short trunk and a dense, usually narrow and oblong crown. When surrounded by woods, red maples are taller and clean of branches for an impressive distance from the ground. The leaves usually have five lobes, although they're not as deeply cut as other types of maples.

The wood of the red maple is soft and not known for its durability. It can be used for furniture or wood pulp, but to my mind, its best use is for beauty and shade. Like the sugar maple, its sap can be used for sugar or syrup. The red maple can be thought of in somewhat heroic terms; when an area is laid waste by fire, this tree often follows the aspen as one of the very first to regrow. In so doing it helps prepare the soil and invites back other wildlife, which in turn helps other trees repopulate. The red maple is a favorite feeding tree for deer, rabbits, and beavers. It can grow in almost any temperate region of the United States.

How to Grow a Red Maple from Seed

APRIL–MAY: Gather fruits from the red maple. These appear on all maples as samaras, which contain the seeds. In shape a samara looks like the propeller of an airplane; on red maples two samaras are fused together to resemble a pair of wings, each approximately one to one and a half inches long. They are green when they first appear, gradually turning red and then reddish brown as they mature. The actual seed is contained in the swollen tip of the samara. Each samara contains one seed, so to grow ten to twenty trees you should collect twenty to forty samaras. They may be collected from the ground or from the tree if they have already started to turn reddish brown.

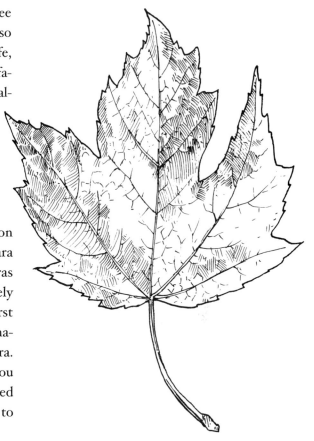

🌿 The best germination occurs when the freshly collected seed is planted immediately in planting trays three to four inches deep filled with loose potting soil. Place the seeds on the soil surface in rows two to three inches apart, then cover with a quarter inch of soil.

🌿 Place the trays in an area with lots of sunlight and temperatures from 72° to 85°F. Use a water-misting bottle to keep the soil just moist. Once the tiny sprouts begin to emerge, incorporate a liquid fertilizer at one-quarter strength for every other watering, and spray weekly with a fungicide to prevent mildew.

JUNE: When the seedlings are two to three inches tall, carefully transplant each one to an individual three- or four-quart growing pot with potting soil. After five days, incorporate the liquid fertilizer at the recommended strength and fertilize once a week.

AUGUST: When the seedlings reach a height of fifteen inches and the trunks are pencil-thick, plant them in the ground. For planting instructions, see page 118.

Where to Plant Your Red Maple

The red maple will grow in a wide range of conditions, including very wet areas and thus can be used to advantage in areas with poor drainage. Unfortunately, the opposite is not true. The only condition it doesn't tolerate well is drought. It is native to swampy areas in the Gulf Coast states and grows nicely throughout the East. It grows quickly and has no serious pests. The red maple is amenable to both sun and shade and will thank you for helping it get started with fertilizer, mulch, and weed removal from around the base. It should do well anywhere in your yard.

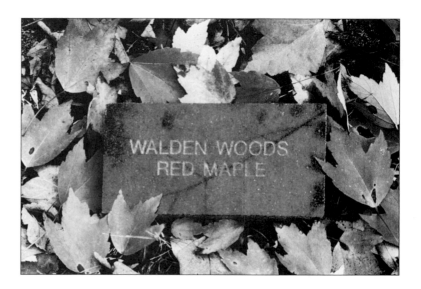

Many people who plant special trees—or who plant a tree for a special reason—like to affix a marker, such as this granite one at Walden Woods.

11
GETTYSBURG ADDRESS
HONEY LOCUST

As THE TRAIN left Washington around noon on November 18, 1863, Abraham Lincoln wasn't feeling well. Yet he was jovial with the others who had joined him on the four-car presidential train: three members of his cabinet, his secretaries, his manservant, the marine band, and a military escort from the Invalid Corps. It was almost a given: the weightier the occasion, the funnier the president's jokes. He took things so seriously, he desperately needed humor to keep a balance.

Now Lincoln's thoughts turned to the event ahead. The main speaker was Edward Everett, former president of Harvard, U.S. senator, and secretary of state. The president had been invited to make a few remarks after Everett's, and he had already written part of his short speech on a piece of White House stationery. As the train gathered speed in the Virginia countryside, the lanky statesman excused himself to write the other half.

Why was this trip so important? He was on his way to Gettysburg, Pennsylvania, the site of one of the bloodiest battles of the Civil War, which had been fought back in the heat of July. The thousands of soldiers killed in battle had been hastily identified and buried and the war moved on; now they were being interred in a more befitting way, and the cemetery was being dedicated.

Lincoln had never been to Gettysburg, but he felt he knew every field and knoll; the dispatches he'd read over those three endless days of battle were forever engraved in his memory. Even at the time, the leaders on both sides had known it would be a decisive battle. It was the Confederacy's first real attempt to claim northern soil; if the Rebels succeeded, the war would turn in their direction. If the North was able to rout them, it would be a different story.

COMMON NAME: HONEY LOCUST

SCIENTIFIC NAME: *Gleditsia triacanthos*

AKA: Confederate pintree, honeyshucks, thorny locust

Perhaps a man's character is like a tree, and his reputation like its shadow; the shadow is what we think of it; the tree is the real thing.

ABRAHAM LINCOLN

The First Pennsylvania
Cavalry Regiment
monument at Gettys-
burg battlefield.

The Union soldiers had won, but at such a price: 23,000 Northerners and 20,000 Southerners lay dead at the end of the brutal battle.

Why?

Lincoln knew the spiritual and emotional cost of the loss of a son, a father, a brother. His *why* demanded an answer, and he planned to give one, to the best of his ability, the next day at Gettysburg. He wanted to explain that the war was not just about preserving the union of the states, it was about the equality of all men; they would fight not just until all states were reunited, but until slavery was abolished from U.S. soil.

These remarks were so significant to him that he had planned the day as carefully as possible. He had even called in William Saunders, the landscape architect in charge of the Gettysburg cemetery, to better understand its topography.

One of the welcome things he had learned was that he would be speaking near a large honey locust tree. Lincoln loved trees; they spoke of home to him. The political pundits of his party bestowed some sort of memorable "tag" on every successful candidate, such as Andrew Jackson's "Old Hickory," and they had searched for one for Abe when he was running for president. When a close friend spoke eloquently of Lincoln's skill with an ax, and of how many rails they had split for cabins and fences, Lincoln became known as "the railsplitter." The term spoke of his rustic beginnings, of the hard work that characterized the pioneer spirit, declaring that he was a man of the people, not a member of the gentry. And it had helped him get elected.

Indeed, Lincoln had split his share of rails back in Illinois and Kentucky; a good number of them had been honey locusts. It had even been said of young Abe that he often preferred the company of trees to that of people. And, visiting a Civil War battlefield, Lincoln had noted the similarity between men and trees, saying he liked trees best when they were not in leaf, as their anatomy could be studied.

The day of the Gettysburg Address was overcast; the honey locust was devoid of leaves and cast no shadow. It was time, on the battlefield that had seen so much loss of life, for "the real thing." Edward Everett spoke for two hours, which was not uncommon in those days, and the audience was appreciative. They were just stretching, and a photographer was setting up his tripod, when Lincoln stood and began to speak. His remarks were so brief that when he finished and sat down, most of the audience wasn't sure whether he'd actually started his speech yet. There was applause, some heartfelt, some confused. But the reporters who were there had an inkling of what they'd just heard, and the full text of the

The Gettysburg Address

Fourscore and seven years ago our fathers brought forth on this continent, a new nation, conceived in Liberty, and dedicated to the proposition that all men are created equal.

Now we are engaged in a great civil war, testing whether that nation or any nation so conceived and so dedicated, can long endure. We are met on a great battle-field of that war. We have come to dedicate a portion of that field, as a final resting place for those who here gave their lives that that nation might live. It is altogether fitting and proper that we should do this.

But in a larger sense, we cannot dedicate—we cannot consecrate—we cannot hallow—this ground. The brave men, living and dead, who struggled here, have consecrated it, far above our poor power to add or detract. The world will little note, nor long remember what we say here, but it can never forget what they did here. It is for us, the living, rather, to be dedicated here to the unfinished work which they who fought here have thus far so nobly advanced. It is rather for us to be here dedicated to the great task remaining before us—that from these honored dead we take increased devotion to that cause for which they gave the last full measure of devotion—that we here highly resolve that these dead shall not have died in vain—that this nation under God shall have a new birth of freedom—and that government of the people, by the people, for the people shall not perish from the earth.

The Gettysburg
Address Honey
Locust in leaf.

speech was soon reprinted. And reprinted. In fact, Lincoln's words were so well chosen and so moving that the Gettysburg Address quickly became one of the hallmark speeches in American history.

War and Peace

I am one of those people who is endlessly fascinated by analysis of our devastating and destructive Civil War. To me, there is something terribly moving about visiting Gettysburg, where so many husbands, fathers, and sons lost their lives; it's a haunting place.

One thing that has always intrigued me about battle strategies at a time when no one had radar or aerial reconnaissance is the important part trees played in battle. They were often used as markers: the objective of the day was to take a certain stand of trees. Or they were used as meeting places: after the attack, we'll all rally at this certain tree.

Trees were also used as lookout posts: before the advent of airplanes, both sides would send scouts up tall trees to gather reports about which battalions were attacking from where, to see how the battle was going, and to have an overall view of the battlefield.

When I stand beneath the Gettysburg Address Honey Locust, near where Lincoln spoke, two thoughts always assail me: first, amazement that this tree, or any battlefield tree, is still standing. Trees were often casualties of warfare, chopped down by either side to fortify the trenches as the soldiers moved toward barricaded trench warfare.

Second, somehow the aura of Abraham Lincoln and what he said that November day does give meaning to the deaths on that battlefield. Because of Lincoln's words and his great caring for the soldiers on both sides, perhaps the occupants of those countless graves can rest in peace.

The Honey Locust

The honey locust (*Gleditsia triacanthos*) is a medium-sized tree with deciduous leaves and zigzag twigs that are covered with thorns. While the thorns make it less than perfect for climbing, it is a hearty, beautiful tree. Another plus is that if you're a novice at planting trees from seed, this one is practically foolproof. Once when Anne and I were cleaning out our refrigerator we found in the back some seedpods from a honey locust that had been there for at least five years. (Usually we keep the back of our refrigerator absolutely sparkling and spotless, I assure you.) Anyway, just out of curiosity, we planted the seeds—and they grew!

The flattened beanlike pods that contain the seeds are long and curved and quite distinctive. Perhaps the tree got its name because the thin pulp of the pods has a sweetish taste. The tree is often used as a shade or ornamental tree; its small yellow flowers are dainty and pretty in the spring. It grows naturally in bottomlands or on slopes where the soil has a high limestone content. The wood is hard, heavy, and strong and has been used for rails, posts, railroad ties, hubs of wheels, and furniture.

How to Grow a Honey Locust from Seed

OCTOBER: Gather the fruits from a honey locust tree. They appear on the tree as pods, which are at first green, turning orange to reddish brown when ripe and gradually turning brown as they dry. They are about five to eight inches long, one-half to one inch long, and flat, with slightly raised areas where the seeds lie within. The seeds are small, black, round with flat sides, and extremely hard. To grow ten to twenty trees, collect two to four pods, as there are approximately ten seeds per pod. These pods stay on the tree well into December, and the seeds will still be good then.

❧ Place the pods in an open container and set it in a warm, dry room to dry; when completely dried the outer pod coat will be papery to the touch. The dried pods should be easy to split. Just tear one end, pull apart the two halves of the pod, and remove the seeds. Store them in a resealable plastic bag in the vegetable storage bin of the refrigerator at a temperature setting of 35° to 43°F for sixty to ninety days.

FEBRUARY: Remove the seeds from the refrigerator. Due to the hardness of the seed coat, the seeds must be boiled to soften them

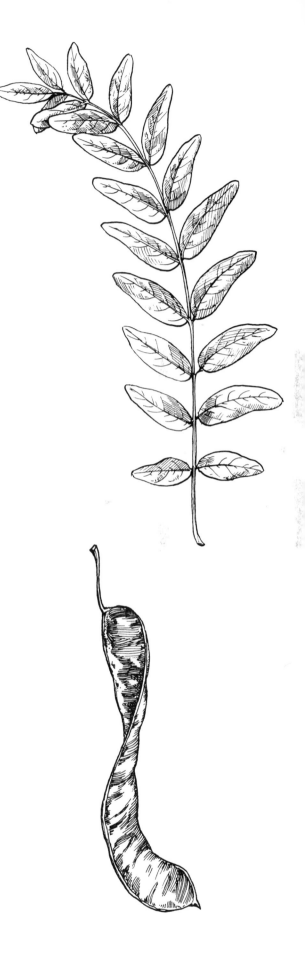

enough for germination. Fill a saucepan with water and bring to a boil. Add the seeds and submerge them for approximately one minute, then remove the saucepan from the heat and let the seeds soak overnight in the gradually cooling water. The next morning they should be swollen and ready to plant.

🐝 Prepare planting trays three to four inches deep filled with loose potting soil. Remove the seeds from the water and place them on the soil surface in rows two to three inches apart, then cover with a half inch of soil.

🐝 Place the trays in an area protected from freezing, with lots of sunlight and temperatures from 72° to 85°F. Use a water-misting bottle to keep the soil just moist. Once the tiny sprouts begin to emerge, incorporate a liquid fertilizer at one-fifth strength for every other watering, and spray weekly with a fungicide to prevent mildew.

MAY: When the seedlings are two to three inches tall, carefully transplant each one to an individual three- or four-quart growing pot with potting soil. After five days, incorporate the liquid fertilizer at the recommended strength and fertilize once a week. Honey locust seedlings are slow growers, so they will need to remain in the growing pots over the first winter.

MARCH: When the seedlings reach a height of fifteen inches and the trunks are pencil-thick, plant them in the ground. For planting instructions, see page 118.

Where to Plant Your Honey Locust

The honey locust is native to rich, fertile soils along creeks and streams, but it will thrive almost anywhere. It's very drought-resistant and will tolerate alkaline or acid soil as well as extreme heat and extreme cold. Its shady crown allows light to filter through, so shrubs or grass can easily be grown beneath its umbrella-shaped crown. This tree grows quickly and prefers a sunny spot.

A THORNY MATTER

The honey locust is considered an excellent landscape tree, but it has endured a bad rap for the numerous long thorns it drops to the ground that can easily pierce shoe leather! A friendlier, thornless honey locust was found and propagated many years ago, nearly eliminating this tree's most objectionable trait. However, the original honey locust, thorns and all, can still be found in its natural setting.

12
FREDERICK DOUGLASS WHITE OAK

FROM DOWNTOWN WASHINGTON today, if you look to the southwest, you can see a beautiful house atop a hill with sweeping vistas, and in its front yard the unmistakable form of a stately white oak. In 1877 this house, in an all-white area, was purchased by a former slave. It seems completely fitting that such a fine tree and property were owned by Frederick Douglass; overcoming obstacles was his stock in trade.

As a bright young slave in 1826, Frederick Augustus Washington Bailey, age eight, was taught how to read by his owner, the upstanding Mrs. Hugh Auld of Baltimore, Maryland. She deliberately and purposefully became a lawbreaker by teaching her houseboy. When her husband discovered what she'd done, he halted the tutoring sessions immediately, believing (as many did) that education made blacks unfit for slavery, if not downright dangerous. Frederick continued his learning as best he could with the aid of local schoolboys whom he would meet in the streets.

The youngster was used to fending for himself. The son of a slave woman and an unidentified white man, Frederick was taken from his mother in infancy and never knew his father. He was raised by his grandmother on the Wye Plantation on Maryland's Eastern Shore, where he was a favorite and deemed suitable to be sent to the Aulds as a houseboy. Unfortunately, the Aulds found him too independent, and when he was sixteen, Frederick was sent back to the plantation. Soon after his return, he was sent to work for Edward Covey, a "slave breaker" who specialized in shattering the spirit of rebellious slaves. Frederick had gone from being a house slave held in relatively high regard to being a field hand who did backbreaking work from dawn to dusk in the heat of the sun and in howling winter winds. To protest or even rest invited harsh beatings or other cruelties.

COMMON NAME: WHITE OAK

SCIENTIFIC NAME: *Quercus alba*

AKA: American oak, ridge white oak, fork-leaf oak, stave oak

STATE TREE: Maryland, Illinois, Connecticut

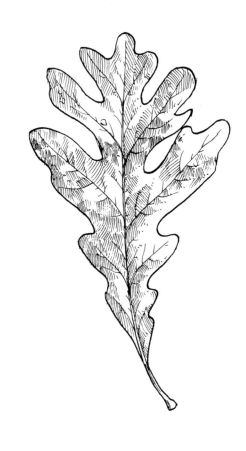

The Wye Plantation, on Maryland's Eastern Shore, where Frederick Douglass spent most of his childhood, is home to the largest white oak in the United States. At last measure, it stood a majestic ninety-six feet tall.

Young Frederick couldn't stand the horrible conditions of his life, and within months he organized three other young slaves in an escape attempt. Before they could get away, they were discovered and punished severely.

This merely stoked his desire for freedom, and five years later his carefully laid plan was a success. He managed to flee to New York City, and then to Bedford, Massachusetts, where he changed his name to Frederick Douglass to elude the slave hunters. He found work as a laborer and married Anna Murray. Together they sought to become known as a respectable family in Bedford and to raise their children in peace.

But fate, and Douglass's own gifts and personality, decreed another path. In 1841 he was asked to speak to an antislavery conven-

The white oak towers above Frederick Douglass's home in Washington, D.C.

tion in Nantucket. There the other attendees discovered something shocking: they had an unparalleled orator in their midst, a black former slave who could give voice to the faceless suffering of so many. Undoubtedly, Frederick himself was surprised by the effect of his words. By all accounts, he returned from Nantucket a changed man; no longer a silent laborer, he had found a cause. As a professional spokesman for the Massachusetts Anti-Slavery Society, he was not just helping three of his brother slaves escape; he would help liberate millions.

It was hard for many to believe that such an eloquent speaker had ever been a slave. To counter these accusations, Douglass wrote an autobiography, *The Life and Times of Frederick Douglass,* in which he named his former master and the plantation on which he'd grown up. Bounty hunters were soon on his trail, so he embarked upon an extended book tour in Great Britain. When he returned two years later, he had enough money to buy his own freedom.

He began an antislavery newspaper, the *North Star,* and during the Civil War he served as an adviser to President Lincoln. After the war he moved from Rochester, New York, to Washington, D.C. There he worked for full civil rights for freed men and extended his beliefs to include women, wholeheartedly joining the women's rights movement.

His appointments became ever more prominent: he was assistant secretary of the Santa Domingo Commission in 1871, a marshal of the District of Columbia, and recorder of deeds. He then was appointed U.S. minister and consul general to Haiti, the first former slave to hold such an important position.

In 1877 his intelligence served him well again. Through a bank he was working with, he learned that one of the most beautiful properties in the District of Columbia was in bankruptcy and would be offered at a bank sale. Moving quickly, he purchased the property, had all the papers signed, and moved in well before the members of the white community realized what had happened. As shocked as some of them may have been, Douglass was an important man by then and there was little they could do. Frederick happily named his new home Cedar Hill because the property was graced with many trees. It also sat on one of the highest hills in Washington, with a commanding view of the Capitol—it was by far the nicest house in the neighborhood.

One of Cedar Hill's largest trees, and one of Douglass's obvious favorites, is a beautiful white oak that stands proudly in the front of the lawn. I have been to Cedar Hill, which is now a National Historic Site, many times. If you're walking up to it from

Frederick Douglass's great-great-grandson, Kevin Douglass Greene, at Cedar Hill.

the Capitol, the white oak is the first thing you see—and it can be seen standing tall from a long way off.

I like to imagine Frederick Douglass and his family coming out to sit in the oak tree's shade on hot summer days, Douglass bringing his beloved violin and entertaining both family and guests with some lively music. Another scene from Douglass's life played out under this tree as well. One cold February day in 1895, he wasn't feeling well. He left a women's rights meeting, which was being led by his friends Susan B. Anthony and Elizabeth Cady Stanton, and walked home to Cedar Hill. There in the yard he had a heart attack and sat down for his final rest beneath his beloved tree.

THE LEGACY ENDURES

The fact that that this white oak witnessed Frederick Douglass's moments of joy and his important meetings and stood over him at his death moves me each time I visit Cedar Hill. In the course of working with this tree, I've had the good fortune to become friends with Frederick Douglass's great-great-grandson, Kevin Douglass Greene. An energetic, idealistic man, Kevin truly carries his famous ancestor's mantle proudly. He is a recruiter for the U.S. Army, and his work allows him to reiterate Frederick's beliefs. Following what many would consider a grueling schedule, he visits schools all across the United States, talking about what his great-great-grandfather did and why civil and human rights are still so important for all of us.

A man after my own heart, Kevin makes sure to leave a marker at each school he visits to serve as a remembrance of the occasion, a memorial to his great-great grandfather, and a reminder to respect each person. How does he do that? At each school he visits, he plants a tree. His legacy, too, will long be remembered.

THE WHITE OAK

The white oak (*Quercus alba*) is a slow-growing but long-lived, majestic tree. The average white oak will grow to sixty or eighty feet tall, but in old-growth forests, it's not unusual to find them over one hundred feet tall, having lived for three to five centuries! The leaves are from five to nine inches long and are distinguished by the number of lobes—usually seven.

The wood of the white oak has long been valued as a high-grade all-purpose wood. It's heavy, tough, and hard, with a close

WORTH THE WAIT

Although you may have to wait ten to twelve years to see acorns on your white oak, once you do, look out. This tree may produce more than 10,000 acorns annually over the course of its long life, possibly 350 to 400 years. Luckily, these sweet acorns are a dietary staple for over eighty species of birds and mammals, just as they were to Native Americans and early European settlers, who boiled the acorns and ground them into flour. So nary an acorn goes to waste.

grain, perfect for fine furniture and flooring. In the past it was used to build ships and to make barrels, wagons, and railroad ties as well as for fuel.

How to Grow a White Oak from Seed

October: Gather the fruits, or acorns, from a white oak tree. The acorns are one to one and a half inches long, oblong to oval in shape, green at first, turning tan-brown as they ripen, and topped with a corky overcap that is scaly in appearance. Acorns can be gathered from the tree, but they must be fully ripe, showing no green color. Or you can collect them from the ground, but don't take any that have tiny weevil holes or that feel hollow. Each fruit contains one seed, so for ten to twenty trees, gather twenty to forty acorns. If you float the acorns in a bucket of water, the best ones will sink; discard those that float.

☙ Leave the acorns in an open container and allow them to dry completely, which should take only a few days. Then remove the scaly overcap and keep only the actual acorn, being careful not to puncture the seed coat. Plant the acorns immediately in planting trays three to four inches deep filled with loose potting soil, then cover with a half inch of soil.

Place these trays in an area protected from freezing, with lots of sunlight and temperatures from 72° to 85°F. Use a water-misting bottle to keep the soil just moist. Once the tiny sprouts begin to emerge, incorporate a liquid fertilizer at one-quarter strength for every other watering, and spray weekly with a fungicide to prevent mildew.

MAY: When the seedlings are two to three inches tall, carefully transplant each one to an individual three- or four-quart growing pot with potting soil. After five days, incorporate liquid fertilizer at the recommended strength and fertilize once a week.

AUGUST: When the seedlings reach a height of fifteen inches and the trunks are pencil-thick, plant them in the ground. For planting instructions, see page 118.

Mighty oaks from little acorns grow.

Where to Plant Your White Oak

A white oak grown in the open, unhampered by neighboring trees, will in old age attain a marvelous spread, with a wide and welcoming crown consisting of massive horizontal branches, often twisted rather than straight. It is a beautiful and stately tree, a lovely addition to any property. You should plant it where it will have room to stretch and grow into its glory. The tree is perfect for large yards, parks, and golf courses. If you want an ornamental shade tree to park a bench under, this is the perfect candidate. Because it needs solid, deep roots, the only place it doesn't do well is in an urban setting where the soil is very shallow or abused. It thrives on rich, moist soil but also does well where soil and moisture are only fair. If you fertilize and irrigate it, the tree will certainly thrive. The white oak is a slow grower but it will last for generations. Planting one is a great way to leave your mark on this earth.

Natural Powers

White oak bark has been used by Native American cultures for hundreds of years to treat wounds and intestinal problems. One of the strongest natural astringent botanicals available, the bark possesses powerful anti-inflammatory and antiseptic properties as well. Rich in tannins, vitamin B_{12}, and minerals such as calcium, iron, and zinc, white oak bark tightens tissues, strengthens blood vessels, and alleviates inflammation and irritations caused by poor digestion, ulcers, strep throat, and skin conditions.

13
Wyatt Earp Black Walnut

My pathways to boyhood adventure in Iowa were the outdoors and books. I read all the usual favorites, from the Hardy Boys adventures to Mark Twain's books, until I discovered my all-time favorite author, Louis L'Amour. I especially loved L'Amour's books about real historical figures, the Wild West, and frontier days.

Of course, the myths of the Wild West often had a basis in fact, in the lives and stories of real men and women. You can imagine my boyhood excitement when I discovered that one of the most famous lawmen of all time, Wyatt Earp, had grown up in Iowa, too, in the town of Pella, though he and his older brothers had been born in Monmoth, Illinois, in the decades before the Civil War. (Their birthplace still stands and is open to the public.) Although their father wasn't thrilled about fighting for "the government," he did not keep his three oldest sons from enlisting to fight for the union; he himself stayed home in Pella, training and recruiting troops.

For most of his life, Wyatt Earp prided himself on being able to resolve situations with his wits rather than his fists. In many ways he truly represented the mythical hero of the Old West. He is most famous as a lawman in Dodge City and Tombstone, Arizona. He was also a farmer, stage coach driver, boxing promoter, church deacon, saloon keeper, gambler, prospector, bounty hunter, and even a Wells Fargo agent. In every role, he was bound by his own code of honor.

In Wichita, Kansas, he got into a fistfight with a hotel owner named Doc Black, whom he felt was mistreating a young boy. Earp knocked out Black without much trouble and was arrested. Down at the jail, the marshal and the mayor together decided that any-

COMMON NAME:

BLACK WALNUT

SCIENTIFIC NAME: *Juglans nigra*

AKA: American black walnut, burbank walnut, gunwood, Virginia walnut

one who could handle Doc Black—who was known for having a temper only slightly less fierce than his wife's—would make a good peace officer, and Earp was hired.

He was celebrated for his honesty as a lawman. On one occasion he hauled in a stranger who had collapsed in a drunken stupor carrying a large roll of cash. When he was released the next day, he still had every penny, less his fine. This was so unusual at the time that it was noted in the news.

In Dodge City, Earp got to know another Doc—Doc Holliday. During the 1870s and early '80s, most of the Earp family and Doc Holliday ended up in Tombstone, Arizona, a wild and woolly town that was far from the train line to New York. Virgil Earp was the marshal in town, and a feud had developed between the Earp brothers and a gang led by Ike Clanton. The celebrated end of that feud was the infamous gunfight at the O.K. Corral, in which three of the Clanton gang ended up dead. The townspeople discharged Virgil Earp, believing the town marshal had overstepped his bounds.

Less than a year later another Earp, Morgan, was murdered. The remaining Earp brothers took the law into their own hands and avenged his death, and Wyatt Earp was forced to flee a murder charge. He moved on to Colorado and then to California, always feeling that his many accomplishments would be forever overshadowed by those two minutes at the O.K. Corral.

In 1907 Bat Masterson wrote of him:

> Wyatt Earp is one of the few men I personally knew in the West in the early days whom I regarded as absolutely destitute of physical fear … I believe he values his own opinion of himself more than that of others, and it is his own good report that he seeks to preserve … He never in his career resorted to the pistol excepting in cases where such a course was absolutely necessary.

THE MONEY TREE

Black walnut trees grow slowly, so the annual rings are very dense. When harvested, the wood has an attractive burl, and because of its density it can be planed into thin, decorative veneers like those found in luxury cars. Hybrid species that claim to be fast-growing can't be used in this way.

Black walnut trees grow best if undisturbed and far from developed areas. The wood is now scarce and valuable, so some farsighted planters have established groves of these trees to be harvested as money crops by their grandchildren.

THE BLACK WALNUT

I've always thought it great that Wyatt Earp was born in what passed for a typical suburban house—1848-style, of course—in Monmouth, Illinois. The curators of the Wyatt Earp Birthplace have reported that some visitors are disappointed when they see it for the first time, because they're expecting a log cabin or a Wild West shed. But even famous gunslingers had to start somewhere, and a quiet street in an Illinois town suited Earp just fine. Years

These huge walnuts, the size of tennis balls, were gathered by Bob and Melba Matson, who live in the Wyatt Earp home in Monmouth, Illinois. Mrs. Matson said the walnuts were the largest the tree had ever produced.

later he would remember Monmouth well—the fences almost too high for him to climb, the wild spaces that needed investigating, the streams and rivers that charted courses to adventure. And it was in Monmouth, in a little clapboard house shaded by a stately black walnut, that the lifelong journey of a legend began.

Oddly, the beginning of my own journey was marked by black walnut trees (*Juglans nigra*). In the yard of our second home in Amana stood a magnificent black walnut that had been planted forty years earlier by my uncle. The walnut is a slow-growing tree, and from the moment I first studied that tree in our yard, I understood that my uncle had not planted this tree for himself but for future generations. For me. And I appreciated it.

So it wasn't by accident that Uncle Buddy and I planted walnut trees in our sojourn along the river. At the time we understood we were doing a good deed for the generations who would come along after we were gone. That selfless attitude is one I've seen reflected again and again in tree planters. We're a good group of folks!

My first real job was as a clean-up boy at the Amana Furniture Company. I would go in after all the carpenters and woodworkers had left for the day and sweep up the wood shavings. I learned right away that the coarse-grained black walnut wood, so slow to grow, was prized above all others for serious woodworking. I loved the texture and smell of its shavings as I swept them together. They always stood out to me.

The black walnut has fern-shaped leaves, usually three to five inches long, which provide a lot of shade. The tree will bear only a few nuts if planted alone. However, if you plant several within thirty to fifty feet of each other, they will cross-pollinate and produce a bumper crop.

Black walnut trees eventually grow sixty to eighty feet tall, growing fastest when young, then slowing considerably. The walnuts from wild trees have hard, thick shells, but those from cultivated trees are much easier to crack. The flavor of the nut is rich and memorable.

HOW TO GROW A BLACK WALNUT FROM SEED

OCTOBER: Gather the fruits, which are two- to three-inch-long nuts, from the black walnut tree. The nuts are round and covered in a thick husk that is green at first, turning dark brown to black as the nut ripens and the husk dries out. The nuts must be gathered before this point, though, because once the husk is dry it is impossible to remove. The best stage for harvesting is when the husk is green and somewhat pliable to the touch. The actual seed lies protected within the hard nutshell. Each nut contains one seed, so for ten to twenty trees, gather twenty to forty nuts.

Once you've gathered the nuts, immediately remove the green husk. The best method is to cut through it with a sharp knife and peel it away from the shell. Place the nuts in a large, resealable plastic bag. In a large bowl, mix three cups of coarse-grade perlite with three cups of water so that it is thoroughly moist. With a slotted spoon, add the drained perlite to the nuts in the bag and lightly toss to thoroughly mix. Mark the date on the bag, seal it tight, and put it in the vegetable storage bin of the refrigerator at a temperature of 40° to 44°F. The nuts will need to remain in the refrigerator for 90 to 120 days.

Check the nuts every second week, looking for mold. If mold appears, rinse the nuts in a ten-to-one solution of water and household bleach, mix with a new batch of moist perlite, and reseal in a new plastic bag, dated with the original date.

FEBRUARY: By now the nuts should have been in refrigeration for 90 to 120 days, and it is time to transfer them to planting trays three to four inches deep filled with loose potting soil. Remove the nuts from the perlite and place them on the soil surface in rows two to three inches apart, then cover with soil a quarter inch deep.

Place the trays in an area protected from freezing, with lots of sunlight and temperatures from 72° to 85°F. Use a water-misting

bottle to keep the soil just moist. The nutshells will eventually rot away from the seeds. Once the tiny sprouts begin to emerge, incorporate a liquid fertilizer at one-quarter strength for every other watering, and spray weekly with a fungicide to prevent mildew.

MAY: When the seedlings are two to three inches tall, carefully transplant each one to an individual three- or four-quart growing pot with potting soil. After five days, incorporate the liquid fertilizer at the recommended strength and fertilize once a week.

AUGUST: When the seedlings reach a height of fifteen inches and the trunks are pencil-thick, plant them in the ground. For planting instructions, see page 118.

ONE TOUGH NUT

The flavor of black walnut meat is distinctive, somewhat more pungent than that of the common English walnut (which is usually California-grown). It's tasty, but the husk is thicker than the common walnut's, so you've got to work for your dinner. Here's how: Wear rubber or latex gloves to protect your hands from the hard-to-remove dark residue you'll encounter as you remove the husks. After removing the husks, roast the nuts in their shells in a 400° oven for twelve to fifteen minutes to make the shells easier to crack.

Here's something you can make with your hard-earned, savory black walnut meats:

BLACK WALNUTS AND WILD RICE

1 CUP UNCOOKED WILD RICE
¼ CUP BUTTER
½ CUP BLACK WALNUTS
1 CUP SLICED MUSHROOMS
½ CUP ONION
½ CUP CHOPPED GREEN PEPPER
1 TEASPOON CHOPPED GARLIC
KOSHER SALT TO TASTE

Cook the wild rice according to the basic directions. Melt the butter and sauté the black walnuts, mushrooms, onion, green pepper, and garlic for about three minutes, or until the vegetables are slightly soft. Add the wild rice and season to taste with kosher salt; continue cooking, stirring regularly, until the wild rice is heated through. Serves four to six.

Where to Plant Your Black Walnut

Plant your black walnut in full sun, and keep in mind that when mature it may reach eighty to one hundred feet in height, with a forty- to fifty-foot spread. (It does grow slowly, so this may be your grandchild's observation!) This tree needs plenty of moisture and a good nutrient supply to reach its full height, but it can tolerate drought if the soil is good.

Beware the Lumber Pirates

The rich, dark wood of the black walnut tree is extremely good-looking and durable and is highly valued for its use in making furniture, cabinets, gunstocks, paneling, and veneers, among other uses. So valued, in fact, and in such demand, that in some areas of the South and Southwest there are lumber pirates who will sneak onto a property, cut down the black walnut, haul it off, and sell it at a premium to a hardwood lumber company. Why? Because top-quality, mature sawlogs can fetch upward of $5,000 apiece!

Seeds for the Famous & Historic Trees project are gathered by volunteer groups such as scout troops and historical organizations as well as by National Park Service personnel. The collectors watch over the old trees and collect seeds in spring or fall, depending on the species, and send them to our nurseries.

14

Amelia Earhart Sugar Maple

Amelia earhart was a spirited young girl for the early twentieth century. Her pioneering ancestors had settled in Atchison, Kansas, when it was the last outpost of civilization before the Wild West. While her father was in Kansas City trying to eke out a living, Amelia and her younger sister, Muriel, lived with their grandparents on their farm in Atchison, where Amelia was the favorite of the neighborhood and already displaying leadership qualities. "We always waited for her to decide what we were going to do," says her friend Katherine.

Amelia was always full of ideas. In the winter of 1904, the seven-year-old decided to try out the sled she and Muriel had gotten for Christmas. Their grandmother, determined to instill "proper" deportment in the two girls, had instructed them only to ride sitting up, like young ladies. But Amelia wanted *speed*. She surveyed the hill and positioned the sled. Then she ran and threw herself on it, in "belly-slammer" style. Halfway down the hill, going faster by the second, she saw a horse wearing blinders turn onto the road in front of her. The owner, bundled up against the elements, didn't hear her urgent cries. There was nothing to do but go for it. Amelia put her head down and shot straight underneath the horse, coming through unhurt on the other side. Amelia's spin on the story was that had she been sitting, ladylike, she undoubtedly would have been badly injured by the horse.

In 1907 Earhart's father took the entire family to the World's Fair in St. Louis, where Amelia fell in love with the thrill of the roller coaster. When the family returned home, she decided to build one of her own, which she did with the help of Muriel, her pal Ralphie Morton, and her uncle Carl. The whole gang of them attached wooden tracks to the shed and ran them to the lawn

COMMON NAME: Sugar Maple

SCIENTIFIC NAME: *Acer saccharum*

AKA: hard maple, sweet maple, sugartree

STATE TREE: New York, Vermont, West Virginia, Wisconsin

below. They made a cart using buggy wheels to fit the track, which they greased with lard. Then they hauled the cart up to the shed roof, where Amelia lay in it and Muriel held on until Amelia gave the signal to let go. The first run ended in a huge crash landing, but Amelia made some adjustments to the tracks and the second run was a great success. It was, she said, "just like flying."

Amelia always had a great imagination. She adored the stately sugar maple that grew outside her bedroom at the front of the farmhouse and its companion tree, a linden that also grew in front of the house. She named them Philemon and Baucis. In Ovid's *Metamorphoses* the god Jupiter turned Philemon into an oak and Baucis into a linden tree after their deaths so that their branches might be intertwined forever. In my mind's eye I picture Amelia sitting in her bedroom window studying those trees, watching as the propeller-shaped maple seeds gracefully winged their way to earth. While it might be too much to suppose that the maple tree inspired her to take up flying, it is clear that the memories of her happy childhood prepared her well for the challenges she would embrace as a woman.

The second half of her life, of course, is better known. She began to fly in 1920, when it was still an unusual and risky pastime, solely the domain of men. In 1928 she became the first woman to cross the Atlantic by air; in 1932 she became the first woman, and

Amelia Earhart's home in Atchison, Kansas, with the sugar maple that grew outside her window.

Amelia Earhart in
1932.

only the second person, after Charles Lindbergh, to fly the Atlantic solo. She also made the first successful flight to Hawaii from the United States, a longer route than across the Atlantic, and one that had previously ended only in disaster. In 1937 she set out to be the first person to fly around the world. She and her navigator, Fred Noonan, were lost at sea somewhere over the Pacific.

Still, the dreams she dreamed in that Atchison farmhouse had more than come true, and she has inspired untold thousands of hearts in the decades since.

The Sugar Maple

Sugar maples (*Acer saccharum*) hold a special place in my own heart. My family planted one between our house and that of our neighbors the Sandersfields, the same day we planted a linden on the other side with our friends and neighbors the Oehls. I remember how much fun we kids had planting the trees. The sugar maple blew down in a storm a few years ago, but the linden still stands, and Karen Oehl still lives in the same house. She's all grown up, as is the tree—and as I am, I guess. I love to drive past that tree when I'm visiting home. The sugar maple and linden outside my boyhood home felt like my own happy link to Amelia Earhart; they stood in the same position outside my bedroom window as Amelia's trees did outside hers.

I was glad to discover that Amelia loved trees; an environmentalist before her time, she hated seeing any trees cut down. (In the Kansas of her day, she undoubtedly thought they could use a few more!) It even occurred to me that trees and aviators occupy that same unique space between heaven and earth.

After working with trees for so long, I believe that each type has a personality of its own, and in Amelia's beloved sugar maples I see many of her own traits reproduced. For instance, sugar maples are tall and upright; they dislike being crowded and thrive in their own space. (Friends say that although Amelia was friendly and outgoing one on one, the only part of her career she intensely disliked was dealing with the large crowds who came to see her takeoffs and landings.)

Sugar maples are proud, sturdy trees that can live for centuries and grow to heights of fifty or sixty feet. They thrive especially in northern climates, from Canada and Newfoundland down to north Georgia and eastern Texas. Their leaves have the classic five lobes (the Canadian maple leaf is a sugar maple), with moderately deep notches between the lobes. The points of the leaf are firm, not drooping; it is a classic, elegant green leaf.

Every tree gives something back, but perhaps none gives quite as much as the sugar maple. Its blaze of autumn colors is spectacular to see: the bright yellows and deep reds fairly glow.

One of our most valuable hardwood trees, this maple has beautifully grained wood, which makes good lumber and beautiful furniture. But the sugar maple gives us the most as a living, growing tree. Its sap, like blood that courses through its veins, supports many a thriving business in maple tapping and syrup and sugar production. It is one of our country's most important commercial trees.

Keeping promises was very important to Amelia Earhart; many say she took off on that last leg of her ill-fated flight only because she had promised she would and so many people were counting on her. (Her Lockheed had crashed in Hawaii, and she wasn't sure it was up to the grueling flight.) Sugar maples may not make verbal promises, but if you plant one, it will be there for your family for centuries, offering shade and sap, something to count on. It will harbor the dreams of many more young girls and boys who admire its branches from a childhood window.

How to Grow a Sugar Maple from Seed

OCTOBER: Gather the fruits from the sugar maple tree. The fruit of all maple trees is called a samara, whose general shape is like that of an airplane propeller. On sugar maples two samaras are fused together to resemble a pair of wings, each approximately one to two inches long. They are green when they first appear, gradually turning red, then reddish brown as they mature. The actual seed is contained in the swollen tip of the samara. Each samara contains one seed, so to grow ten to twenty trees you should collect twenty to forty samaras. You can collect them from the ground or from the tree if they have already started to turn reddish brown.

Place the samaras in an open container set in the sun and let them dry for several days, until they are completely dry and papery to the touch. Then take a large pot and pour in approximately three to four times as much water as you have seeds. Submerge the seeds and let them soak overnight. The next morning, drain the seeds and place them in a large, resealable plastic bag. In a large bowl, mix three cups of coarse-grade perlite with three cups of water so that it is thoroughly moist. With a slotted spoon, add the drained perlite to the seeds in the bag and lightly toss to thoroughly mix. Mark the date on the bag, seal it tight, and put it in the vegetable storage bin of the refrigerator at a temperature of 40° to 44°F. The seeds will need to remain in the refrigerator for sixty to ninety days.

Check the seeds every second week, looking for mold. If mold appears, rinse the seeds in a ten-to-one solution of water and household bleach, mix with a new batch of moist perlite, and reseal in a new plastic bag, dated with the original date.

JANUARY: By now the seeds should have been in refrigeration for sixty to ninety days, and it is time to transfer them to planting trays three to four inches deep filled with loose potting soil. Remove the seeds from the perlite and place them on the soil surface in rows two to three inches apart, then cover with a half inch of soil.

Place the trays in an area protected from freezing, with lots of sunlight and temperatures from 72° to 85°F. Use a water-misting bottle to keep the soil just moist. Once the tiny sprouts begin to emerge, incorporate a liquid fertilizer at one-fifth strength for every other watering, and spray weekly with a fungicide to prevent mildew.

MAY: When the seedlings are two to three inches tall, carefully transplant each one to an individual three- or four-quart growing pot with potting soil. After five days, incorporate the liquid fertilizer at the recommended strength and fertilize once a week.

AUGUST: When the seedlings reach a height of fifteen inches and the trunks are pencil-thick, plant them in the ground. For planting instructions, see page 118.

SUGAR AND SNOW

Hot maple syrup on top of freshly packed snow forms a chewy and delicious treat.

Boil the maple syrup until it thickens, then spread it on spoon-sized mounds of snow. The hot syrup transforms instantly on contact with the snow, creating an unusually sweet and delightful candy.

Or try pouring maple syrup directly onto freshly packed snow and make maple syrup snow-cones.

Where to Plant Your Sugar Maple

Sugar maples like the sun, and they like a little room of their own. They like soil that gets plenty of water and is moist but also has good drainage. This tree is a slow to moderate grower. It does especially well in chillier northern climates. In fact, if it is planted too far south, the warmer weather will produce leaf scorch. If you live in the South, you'll want to consider the Florida maple (*Acer barbatum*) in its place. In the North, though, you can't find a more dramatic or colorful autumn tree than the sugar maple. It's been called the pinup of trees because its lovely shape and color have caused it to grace so many calendar pages. The only thing to really keep in mind is that when the tree is mature, the leaves don't let much sunlight through, so don't plan to grow plants or grass underneath.

The Discerning Leaf Collector

The sugar maple puts on the most gorgeous display of color in the fall, its leaves ranging from yellow to deep crimson to brilliant red and orange. Collecting autumn leaves is one way to bring the beauty of the season indoors.

Bring a composition notebook along on your walk and slip the leaves between the pages to protect them and to keep them from drying out too fast. Choose leaves that have already fallen to the ground, and look for a variety of sizes, shapes, and colors. Select only good, undamaged leaves, and make sure you pick up whole leaf sections, not just leaflets. Jot down the locations of the collected leaves in your notebook, along with the date, time, weather, and other impressions you have as you

walk. The notebook itself can become a leaf journal and memory book that you use from year to year. You can also use the colorful leaves in table settings, mantle decorations, and wreaths.

To press the leaves, keep them in your notebook or lay them flat between layers of newspaper or other porous paper. Weight the paper with bricks or wood blocks. Change the paper every couple of days and keep your leaf collection in a dry, temperate room to prevent mildew. You can also press the leaves between sheets of waxed paper, using an iron at low setting to heat the paper and fasten the sheets together. When the leaves have dried for fifteen days, you can mount them in a collection book.

15
JOHN F. KENNEDY
POST OAK

FIVE-YEAR-OLD Caroline Kennedy spent one April Sunday in 1963 with a school friend who lived in Arlington, Virginia, just across the river from Washington, D.C. The day was so lovely that the friend's parents took the girls to Arlington National Cemetery on an outing. One view particularly impressed the little girl, and when her father and her uncle came to pick her up, she described it to them enthusiastically. Impressed by her description, her father had the limo driver turn around and head back to Arlington National Cemetery.

So it was that President John F. Kennedy, his brother Robert, and Caroline climbed the steps to the original Lee house and stood in awe, looking back toward Washington over the rolling hills, blossoming cherry trees, and one unusually lovely post oak tree. From there they had a sweeping view of the Capitol and the Lincoln Memorial.

"This is so beautiful," John said to Robert. "I could stay here forever."

Nine months later that wish was fulfilled, though not in a way than anyone would have wanted. Of course, on that

COMMON NAME: POST OAK
SCIENTIFIC NAME: *Quercus stellata*
AKA: iron oak

PRESIDENT JOHN F. KENNEDY

sunny April Sunday, President Kennedy had no idea he was choosing his own gravesite. But today he rests beneath that post oak in one of the loveliest spots in Washington. Along with the water and the Eternal Flame, that post oak stands, renewing itself year after year, season after season. Each spring it speaks to the promise of life after death and to the sacrifice made by each American interred at Arlington Cemetery, a sacrifice appreciated and brought to flower daily in the lives of America's people.

ARLINGTON NATIONAL CEMETERY

In 1831 a young army officer named Robert E. Lee married Mary Custis, a descendant of Martha Washington. Mary had inherited a breathtaking 1,100-acre estate crowned by a graceful plantation house called Arlington House. Robert and Mary Lee lived there for thirty years, until the Civil War began in earnest in 1861. That year Robert resigned his army commission rather than face the prospect of having to fight against his native Virginia, which was threatening to secede from the union. The Lees were forced to flee their home, never to return.

The post oak below John F. Kennedy's grave, with Arlington House (the Custis-Lee mansion) in the background.

Federal troops quickly crossed the river to take command of the property, eventually making Arlington House the headquarters of the Army of the Potomac. The next year, when taxes were due, Mary sent a proxy to pay them. The government refused to accept the taxes unless the owner herself appeared, which Mary could not do. The federal government formally seized the property. (After the war, Robert E. Lee's eldest son, George Washington Custis Lee, sued the government for this action. He won and was reimbursed $150,000, the fair market value of the land; in 1882 he handed over the property officially to the United States.)

During the war, 200 acres of the original 1,100 were set aside as a national cemetery. The first burials, of sixty-five soldiers, took place on June 15, 1864. At the time the cemetery was "segregated," which simply meant that enlisted men were buried separately from officers.

Also around that time, Freedman's Village was started on part of the Arlington estate to provide food, housing, education, and employment training for former slaves. More than 3,800 African Americans from the original Freedman's Village are now buried in the cemetery, with the word "civilian" or "citizen" marked determinedly after their names.

Today Arlington National Cemetery has become a place of reverence and honor for the American people. Interred here are soldiers from every war the United States has fought (the remains of some Revolutionary War soldiers have been moved here). Also resting here are people who have made important contributions to this country: Presidents Kennedy and Taft; Supreme Court justices, such as Earl Warren and Oliver Wendell Holmes; explorers, such as Robert E. Peary and Richard Byrd; and space pioneers, such as Dick Scobee and Michael Smith, who lost their lives in the *Challenger* explosion.

Even today there are fifteen funerals daily, Monday through Friday, at the cemetery. It is one of the most visited sites in the Washington area. All those who come here know that every headstone represents a piece of America bought at a dear price.

The many distinguished trees at Arlington National Cemetery add much to its natural beauty. Each spring when they return to life, bursting with flowers and leaves, they remind us how the fruits of those sacrifices enrich our nation, and our lives, every day.

The Post Oak

The post oak is a distinguished ornamental tree that grows well in the lower Plains states. It has a handsome rounded crown and is often as wide as it is tall—growing forty to fifty feet tall, often with a thirty- to forty-foot spread. The top half of the leaf tends to be larger than the bottom, shaping it somewhat like a cross. In the spring the leaves begin dark red, followed by a deep, dark green throughout the summer and a golden yellow brown in autumn, though on some trees the leaves go directly to brown. The post oak

The mighty oaks (genus *Quercus,* derived from the Celtic words for "fine" and "tree") consist of as many as five hundred species that sort themselves into three groups, based on their microanatomy. These groups are the evergreen oaks, the red oaks, and the white oaks. The post oak is a proud and distinctive representative of the white oak group, generally somewhat smaller than the others and with lighter bark, unbristled leaves, and sweet acorns. The red oaks generally have darker bark, spine-tipped leaves, and bitter acorns. The white and red oaks are common in eastern North America. The evergreen, or live, oaks, which are common in the Deep South, feature dark bark, glossy, dark green leaves, and sweetish acorns.

is a wonderful generational tree to plant; it becomes mature at between two hundred and three hundred years and often survives to four hundred years or more.

How to Grow a Post Oak from Seed

OCTOBER: Gather the fruits, the acorns, from the tree. The acorns are oblong to oval in shape, one to one and a half inches long. They are green at first, turning tan-brown as they ripen, and topped with a corky overcap that is scaly in appearance. The acorns must be fully ripe, with no green showing, so you should collect them from the ground, taking care to avoid those that have tiny weevil holes or that feel hollow. Each acorn contains one seed, so for ten to twenty trees, gather twenty to forty acorns.

℞ Place the acorns in an open container and let them dry completely, which should take only a few days. Then remove the scaly overcap and keep only the actual acorn, being careful not to puncture the seed coat. Plant the acorns in planting trays three to four inches deep filled with loose potting soil in rows two to three inches apart, then cover with a half inch of soil.

℞ Place the trays in an area protected from freezing, with lots of sunlight and temperatures from 72° to 85°F. Use a water-misting bottle to keep the soil just moist. Once the tiny sprouts begin to emerge, incorporate a liquid fertilizer at one-quarter strength for every other watering, and spray weekly with a fungicide to prevent mildew.

MARCH: When the seedlings are two to three inches tall, carefully transplant each one to an individual three- or four-quart growing pot with potting soil. After five days, incorporate the liquid fertilizer at the recommended strength and fertilize once a week.

SEPTEMBER: When the seedlings reach a height of fifteen inches and the trunks are pencil-thick, plant them in the ground. For planting instructions, see page 118.

WHERE TO PLANT YOUR POST OAK

This large, slow-growing tree is one of the most forgiving of the oaks. It thrives in fertile, moist soil but can do well in dry (but not desert) conditions. If your yard has poor soil, the post oak is a good choice, and it will reward you heartily for any trouble you take to fertilize and irrigate it. A lovely shade tree, it can be planted almost anywhere with enough room for the root base to support its growth.

THE ULTIMATE TRAIL MIX

The acorns of the post oak provide high-energy food during fall and winter to a wide range of animals, including wild turkeys, white-tailed deer, squirrels, and other woods rodents. These acorns are critical to the diet and overall life cycles of many of these animals, allowing them to fatten quickly in the fall, endure the winter in good health, and ultimately produce healthy young.

16

ELVIS PRESLEY
PIN OAK

It's a distinctly american story, which begins when thirteen-year-old Elvis Aaron Presley moved with his parents from Tupelo, Mississippi, to Memphis, Tennessee. The musical influence of the city of Memphis on young Elvis was significant; there he soaked up rich gospel traditions, as well as the black R&B he couldn't get enough of on historic Beale Street. At eighteen, Elvis was working as a truck driver for an electrical company (he was

COMMON NAME: PIN OAK

SCIENTIFIC NAME: *Quercus palustris*

AKA: Spanish oak, water oak

Young Elvis with his parents, Vernon and Gladys Presley.

studying to become an electrician) and stopped in at the Sun Records studio to see if he could record a song for his mother's birthday. Sam Phillips, who ran the studio, heard him sing and wasn't impressed, but within a few months Elvis was back in the studio recording "That's All Right, Mama," and this time Phillips took notice. He signed Elvis to a contract, and the song was the first of several hits Presley sang for Sun.

His growing popularity attracted the attention of RCA Records, for whom Elvis recorded his first number-one hit, "Heartbreak Hotel." By 1956 he was able to do more than record a song for his mother, Gladys; he was able to buy himself and his parents—who until then had had just barely enough money to get by—a respectable ranch house in East Memphis.

By then Elvis's popularity was exploding. Millions of people tuned in to the *Ed Sullivan Show* to see Elvis perform, and before long the quiet family neighborhood the Presleys had moved into was quiet no more. Soon it was almost impossible for them to return to their home, let alone lead any kind of private life there, due to the press of fans. Elvis was busy touring and recording and had started making films. So he sent his parents, Vernon and Gladys, out with a real estate agent to scout for a house that would allow for more privacy.

Graceland, Elvis Presley's home in Memphis.

There was one house they particularly liked, a lovely, well-known "society" home, built seventeen years earlier by a doctor and his wife, who were now divorcing. The minute Elvis saw it, he fell in love. The house, of course, was Graceland. By that time he was easily in a position to buy the house, outbuildings, and just under fourteen acres for a little more than $100,000.

Whenever I go to Graceland, the first thing that always impresses me is that the house itself is, by modern celebrity standards, very modest. And as Elvis's fortune grew, he certainly could have afforded a much larger house. But Graceland was his home, his center, his refuge. What he especially loved was the acreage, the feeling of space, and the beauty of the landscaping. Behind the iron gate were many graceful trees that added serenity to his private world. Six or eight oaks line the driveway; magnolias, elms and beeches blossom nearby. Walking the grounds, you can't help but get a sense of peace from strolling in the shade of trees that were unmoved by the great and terrible times of Elvis's life.

As that life got crazier and crazier, he treasured the sanctuary of Graceland more and more. In a 1972 interview, he said without irony, "It's very hard to live up to an image." Graceland was where he could be himself. There he surrounded himself with family. When he bought Graceland, he lived in the main house with only his parents and his grandmother. Eventually, he employed dozens of people, many of them extended family. There were always animals on the grounds, especially when Gladys was alive: chickens, peafowl, horses, lots of dogs, even monkeys. (There's one famous story of young Elvis pulling up in a Cadillac with the backseat full of chickens.) Elvis loved cars and motorcycles, of course, and the garages were full of Cadillacs, Lincolns, Harleys, and an old panel truck he used when he wanted to tool around Memphis unnoticed. Especially in the early days, the grounds of Graceland were happy and bustling—and, with all those animals, probably noisy.

Elvis's second cousin, Jimmy Gambill, who still works there today, recalls going home from school each day to Graceland—where his grandfather, Elvis's uncle, manned the gate—and riding a golf cart all over the grounds.

Elvis's life, of course, ended at Graceland. And it was inside the house, several days later, that the private funeral was held. Afterward, as the coffin was being carried out the door, a limb on one of the big oak trees out in front snapped and fell, barely missing the funeral party, but Elvis's friend Lamar didn't miss a beat. "We knew you'd be back," he wisecracked. "Just not this soon."

The Pin Oak

Who doesn't love a pin oak (*Quercus palustris*)? According to a poll in *American Nurseryman* magazine, it is the most popular shade and street tree planted in the United States. It's a pretty, medium-sized tree that will grow to be seventy to eighty feet tall, yet at maturity its trunk will be only two to three feet wide. The trunk is narrower than in some other oaks (such as the bur oak); the upper half to two-thirds of the branches point upward while the bottom ones droop. The pin oak's pretty leaves, three to seven inches long, are deeply lobed (that is, the sections of the leaves are obviously defined), and the acorns are smaller and shallower than those of other oaks. This tree holds some of its leaves all winter.

Oaks are wonderfully useful hardwoods; in fact, they provide about half of the hardwood lumber used annually in the United States. And most oaks that bear acorns are very popular with wildlife: species that enjoy munching on them include songbirds, grouse, prairie chickens, wood ducks, mourning doves, bobwhites, wild turkeys, black bears, whitetail deer, red fox, gray fox, raccoons, opossums, squirrels, and chipmunks. Deer and rabbits snack on its twigs, and porcupines dine on the layer of the trunk that grows just under the bark.

How to Grow a Pin Oak from Seed

OCTOBER: Gather the fruits, the acorns, which are round, half an inch to one inch long, from the tree. The acorns are green at first, turning dark brown as they ripen, and topped with a corky overcap that is scaly in appearance. You can collect them from the tree, but they must be fully ripe, with no green showing. Or you can collect them from the ground, taking care to avoid those that have tiny weevil holes or that feel hollow. Each acorn contains one seed, so for ten to twenty trees, gather twenty to forty acorns.

๛ Place the acorns in an open container and let them dry completely, which should take only a few days. Then remove the scaly overcap and keep only the actual acorn, being careful not to puncture the seed coat. Plant the acorns in planting trays three to four inches deep filled with loose potting soil in rows two to three inches apart, then cover with a half inch of soil.

๛ Place the trays on a sunny windowsill where the temperature is between 72° and 85°F. Use a water-misting bottle to keep the soil just moist. Once the tiny sprouts begin to emerge, incorporate a liquid fertilizer at one-quarter strength for every other watering, and spray weekly with a fungicide to prevent mildew.

MARCH: When the seedlings are two to three inches tall, carefully transplant each one to an individual three- or four-quart growing pot with potting soil. After five days, incorporate the liquid fertilizer at the recommended strength and fertilize once a week.

AUGUST–SEPTEMBER: When the seedlings reach a height of fifteen inches and the trunks are pencil-thick, plant them in the ground. For planting instructions, see page 118.

Where to Plant Your Pin Oak

The pin oak is a sturdy ornamental tree that thrives in sun. Choose a place to plant it where the lower branches can remain near the ground. They grow that way naturally, and the tree doesn't do well if they are cut off. The pin oak is the most sensitive oak tree to alkaline soils. If your soil pH is over 6, you should choose another oak. But in highly acid soil the pin oak will thrive and will do much better than others of its family. It will respond vigorously to fertilization, mulching, or acidifying of the soil to lower the pH level, if that is necessary.

Dead Wood

It's a wonder that that pin oak branch broke as the funeral party passed by at Graceland. The distinctive branching habit of the pin oak is a key feature of its identity. The lower limbs, which are usually dead, droop; the middle limbs reach out horizontally, and the top limbs slant upward. This tree is a popular residential ornamental tree, in part because it transplants easily, has good-looking foliage and a pyramidal crown. But it's also a poor self-pruner; the lower branches don't fall when they die but slowly droop until they wrap around the tree, forming somewhat of a net protecting the trunk below. So the little surprise the pin oak dropped on Elvis's funeral was decidedly uncharacteristic of this species, and certainly a bit of natural punctuation to the event.

17
Moon Sycamore

*T*HERE IS A SYCAMORE tree in Mississippi with a remarkable history. On January 31, 1971, *Apollo 14* was launched to complete the United States' third lunar landing. Aboard with Edgar Mitchell and Alan Shepard, Jr., was Stuart Allen Roosa, known as "Smokey" from the summers he spent as a smoke jumper in the U.S. Forest Service, one of those elite firefighters who jump from airplanes into forests to battle raging blazes.

Shortly after the announcement of this space mission, Roosa was contacted by Ed Cliff, the director of Forest Management Research at the Forest Service, whom he'd known since his firefighting days. Cliff asked if Roosa could take some tree seeds with him as he circled the moon and then bring the seeds back to earth to plant as "moon trees." Roosa enthusiastically agreed. When *Apollo 14* was launched toward the moon, he was carrying several packets of seeds—loblolly pine, sycamore, sweetgum, redwood, and Douglas fir.

After *Apollo 14* returned to earth, everything aboard the spacecraft went through decontamination. In the process all the seed packets blew open, and it looked as though all the seeds had died. Stan Krugman, the U.S. Forest Service staff geneticist, sorted the jumbled seeds and planted them anyway. To everyone's great delight, the seeds sprouted. In 1975, a moon seedling was planted in front of the Forestry Science Building at Mississippi State University.

That seedling, a sycamore that flew into space, is now a mighty tree. Many of its descendant moon trees were planted during the U.S. bicentennial as a tribute to the human spirit and the adventures of the final frontier.

COMMON NAME: SYCAMORE

SCIENTIFIC NAME: *Platanus occidentalis*

AKA: American plane tree, buttonwood, lacewood

(Above) The launch of *Apollo 14,* which took tree seeds to the moon.

Stuart Roosa and I became phone buddies; we chatted on several occasions about his love for trees. In fact, we were planning a tree planting tour in the spring of 1995 to help schoolchildren plant moon sycamores in their hometowns. Sadly, he died the day after Christmas, 1994. Before his death, he expressed his hope that descendants of this tree could encourage Americans to dream as big as the moon, while purposely planting trees to improve the quality of life here on earth.

THE SYCAMORE

The sycamore is one of the few trees known for its distinctive bark. When the tree matures, after about ten years, it sheds its bark in large patches, creating a mottled trunk of cream, tan, and olive. (The fallen bark and leaves make a terrific mulch.) These large, lovely trees can grow to seventy feet tall in their first twenty years—if you want instant shade, this is the tree to plant!

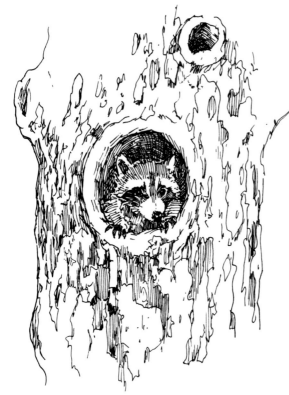

When the dead limb of a sycamore falls off, it creates a home for small animals.

Sycamore wood is hard and coarse. It makes wonderful, slow-burning firewood, for example—*if* you can split it. In pioneer times, the wood's toughness made it popular for wagon wheels, barber poles, and even wooden washing machines. The American sycamore, native to the eastern United States, is a long-lived tree. Philadelphia boasts several sycamores from the days of William Penn.

At maturity, sycamores can reach 110 feet or more, with a spread as wide as their height. The leaves, which may be nearly a foot long, resemble maple leaves, with three to five sharply pointed lobes. The top surface is a medium green; the underside is paler and has hairy veins. The foliage isn't especially colorful when it turns in the autumn, but it will blaze back to glory the following spring, when its round flower clusters, about an inch in diameter, emerge in late May or early June.

Sycamores are trees that give back, even more than most. Wild animals, such as purple finches, squirrels, and foxes, enjoy the seeds. As the branches drop off, most sycamores develop deep cavities that become nesting places for squirrels, bats, and bees.

But sycamores also do a lot for humans. They are great city trees, for they can grow in polluted situations, improving the air quality wherever they are. There are three types of sycamores in the United States: the large American, the smaller Oriental, and the London plane tree. It is the smaller Oriental that is usually planted in urban settings.

Sycamores don't usually need pruning, but in a young tree, pruning can help establish a single central stem.

How to Grow a Sycamore from Seed

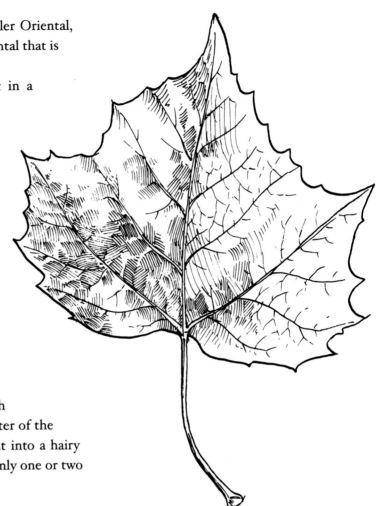

November: Gather fruits from the sycamore tree. The fruits first appear on the tree as one- to one-and-a-half-inch green balls, which will turn brown as they mature. They can be harvested anytime after this transformation. The ball itself is made up of multiple seeds, which are only three-quarters of an inch long and less than a quarter of an inch wide. The portion of the seed closest to the center of the fruit is pointed and hard, and gradually fans out into a hairy tuft. To grow ten to twenty trees you will need only one or two balls, as each ball contains at least twenty seeds.

❧ Place the balls in an open container set in the sun to dry for one to two days. Once they're completely dry you'll be able to easily dislodge the seeds from the fruit ball with firm pressure.

❧ Separate the seeds by continuing to break the ball apart and rubbing each seed until it separates from the ones surrounding it. (The rubbing also will remove the hairy tuft, which is unnecessary for the planting process.) The most important portion of the seed is the hard, pointy tip. Place the seeds in a large, resealable plastic bag. In a large bowl, mix three cups of coarse-grade perlite with three cups of water so that it is thoroughly moist. With a slotted spoon, add the drained perlite to the seeds in the bag and lightly toss to thoroughly mix the seeds with the perlite. Mark the date on the bag, seal it tight, and put it in the vegetable storage bin of the refrigerator at a temperature setting of 40° to 44°F. The seeds will need to remain in the refrigerator for sixty to ninety days.

February: After the seeds have been in refrigeration for sixty to ninety days, it is time to transfer them to planting trays three to four inches deep filled with loose potting soil. Remove the seeds from the perlite and place them on the soil surface in rows two to three inches apart, then cover with one-quarter inch of soil.

❦ Place the trays in an area protected from freezing, with lots of sunlight and temperatures from 72° to 85°F. Use a water-misting bottle to keep the soil moist. Once the tiny sprouts begin to emerge, incorporate a liquid fertilizer at one-quarter strength for every other watering, and spray weekly with a fungicide to prevent mildew.

MARCH: When the seedlings are two to three inches tall, carefully transplant each one to an individual three- or four-quart growing pot filled with potting soil. After five days, use liquid fertilizer at the recommended strength once a week.

AUGUST: When the seedlings reach a height of fifteen inches and the trunks are pencil-thick, plant them in the ground. For planting instructions, see page 118.

WHERE TO PLANT YOUR SYCAMORE

Sycamores are sun lovers; they enjoy a site where they can spread their branches and soak up the sun. They will thrive in a wide range of soil conditions, wet or dry. (If the ground is too dry, buy a bag of potting soil and add it to the planting area to add natural moisture.)

MOON TREES ALL OVER THE WORLD

Because the "moon trees" were southern and western species, not all the states in the Union could plant one as part of the nation's bicentennial celebration. A loblolly pine was planted at the White House, and trees were planted in Brazil and Switzerland and presented as a gift to the emperor of Japan. Moon trees have been planted in Philadelphia, at Valley Forge, in the International Forest of Friendship in Atchison, Kansas, and at various universities and NASA centers. There's even a moon sycamore growing at the Koch Girl Scout Camp in Cannelton, Indiana.

A sycamore seedling in its growing pot.

Ready to be planted outdoors.

 EPILOGUE

IN *The Man Who Planted Trees,* the French writer Jean Giono tells of walking into a desolate area of the Alps beyond Provence in the early part of the twentieth century. The landscape was lifeless, parched, and barren. The remains of the only town sat in ruins, for the spring of water that supported life there had long ago dried up.

As he continued his journey, he came upon the cheerful but solitary dwelling of a shepherd farther up in the hills. The man had dug a deep cistern and had a full garden and a small herd of sheep. The writer spent the night, since the nearest inhabited town was more than a two-day journey away.

That evening the shepherd took out a bag full of acorns and separated out one hundred of the heartiest. The next day the traveler went with him as he planted those seeds. The man told him that since losing both his wife and his son, he'd been planting one hundred trees a day for three years. His name was Elezeard Bouffier and he was content now, at peace with this life. At that point he'd planted 100,000 trees. Of those, 20,000 had sprouted, and 10,000 had become healthy trees.

The writer visited again after the First World War, this time having to travel through a forest to find Bouffier, who was now planting beeches. The local forest department had noticed their unexplained new forest and had turned it into a preserve.

The writer returned again twenty-five years later, after the Second World War. He hardly recognized the landscape. It was full of flora and fauna; the water had returned to the healthy earth. The once-deserted town was now bustling, its houses and businesses rebuilt, the central fountain overflowing. And, of course, beautiful forests surrounded the town, stretching as far as the eye could see.

This parable means a lot to me, because it shows that planting a tree is taking a stand against desolation. It is believing in life and beauty. It is investing in the future.

My fervent hope is that this book will be more to you than an interesting collection of stories about people who love trees. It is meant to be your personal invitation to change the world by planting trees.

It is always fascinating to hear from fellow tree planters about their experiences, whether successful or not. Every tree species reacts differently to climate, season, and weather conditions to produce results as unique as a fingerprint. Let me hear from you! E-mail jeff@historictrees.org or write to American Forests Famous & Historic Trees, 8701 Old Kings Road, Jacksonville, Florida 32219.

This Moreton Bay fig tree growing between Wilshire Boulevard and Rodeo Drive in Beverly Hills, California, has had landmark status since 1930. It serves as a buffer between the commercial and residential areas.

 ## Appendix A

Tree Planting
Information

How to Plant Your Tree Outdoors

Select a planting location, considering the mature height and crown spread of your tree. With a shovel, cut a planting area twelve inches in diameter and six inches deep. Clear all roots, rocks, and weeds from the planting hole. If you have poor soil, mix in Miracle-Gro Garden Soil for Trees and Shrubs.

Remove the tree from the growing container. The best way to preserve the tender roots is to turn the container over into your palm and squeeze the container sides until the entire root ball is free but intact. Place the tree in the center of the planting hole and as deep as the soil level in the growing container. Backfill the hole with soil. Tamp firmly and build a low wall of soil around the outer edge to act as a water ring.

Water the planting area thoroughly. Apply fertilizer in tablet form or spread

Trees span— and connect— generations.

Osmocote Plant Food 14-14-14 evenly on the soil surface. Place four inches of mulch over the entire planting area, but not against the trunk of the tree. Support your tree with a treated stake and plant tape.

At the Famous & Historic Tree Nursery, we let our trees grow to twelve inches before shipping them to customers. The trees come with a planting kit that has proven to be excellent for long-term success. The most important part of the kit is the growing tube. Developed in England, the tube acts like a small greenhouse. It insulates the tree from extreme temperatures; encourages a single straight trunk; accelerates growth as the tree grows toward the

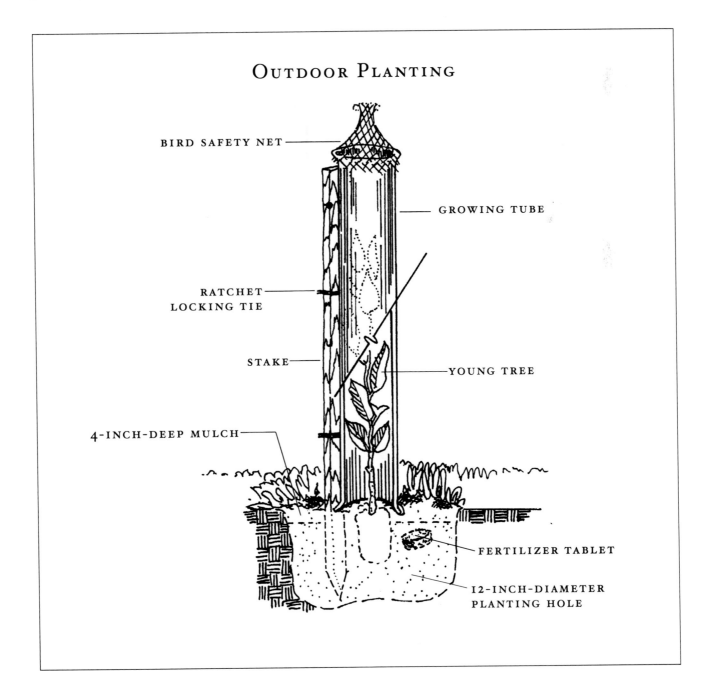

OUTDOOR PLANTING

BIRD SAFETY NET

GROWING TUBE

RATCHET LOCKING TIE

STAKE

YOUNG TREE

4-INCH-DEEP MULCH

FERTILIZER TABLET

12-INCH-DIAMETER PLANTING HOLE

Children marvel at
the growth of their
trees.

light; and provides protection from grazing animals, especially deer.

The tube is placed over the tree, seated into the ground, then staked firmly. We recommend that you leave the tree in the tube until the trunk has developed enough to support the tree without additional staking. Staking can harm young trees by girdling the trunk and cutting into the bark, inviting pests and disease.

These tubes are not easy to find, but if you call or e-mail me, I will send one to you. You'll be a believer after you try it!

Water is essential to establishing a healthy root ball. For the first three months that the tree is in the ground, water it with three gallons every other day unless it has rained. After the tree is established, water during times of drought. Don't allow weeds to grow around your young tree, for they will rob it of essential nutrients and water. Each spring, fertilize your tree (I prefer Miracle-Gro Tree Spikes), change the mulch, and prune any undesirable branches.

Tree Selection Chart

	Flower	Fall Color	Alkaline Soil	Wet Soil	Dry Soil	Height in Feet	Spread in Feet	Rate of Growth*
Apple	•		•			20	15	M
Black walnut			•		•	60	45	S
Bur oak			•		•	60	30	S–M
Cottonwood		•	•	•	•	90	50	F
Honey locust	•		•		•	40	25	M
Live oak			•		•	50	75	S–M
Osage orange		•	•		•	50	30	F
Pecan		•			•	60	40	S–M
Pin oak		•		•	•	70	40	M
Post oak		•			•	40	40	S
Red maple		•			•	40	30	M
Southern magnolia	•			•	•	50	40	S–M
Sugar maple		•		•	•	60	50	M
Sycamore			•	•	•	75	40	F
Tulip poplar		•		•	•	50	30	F
White oak		•		•		70	50	S–M

* S = slow
M = medium
F = fast

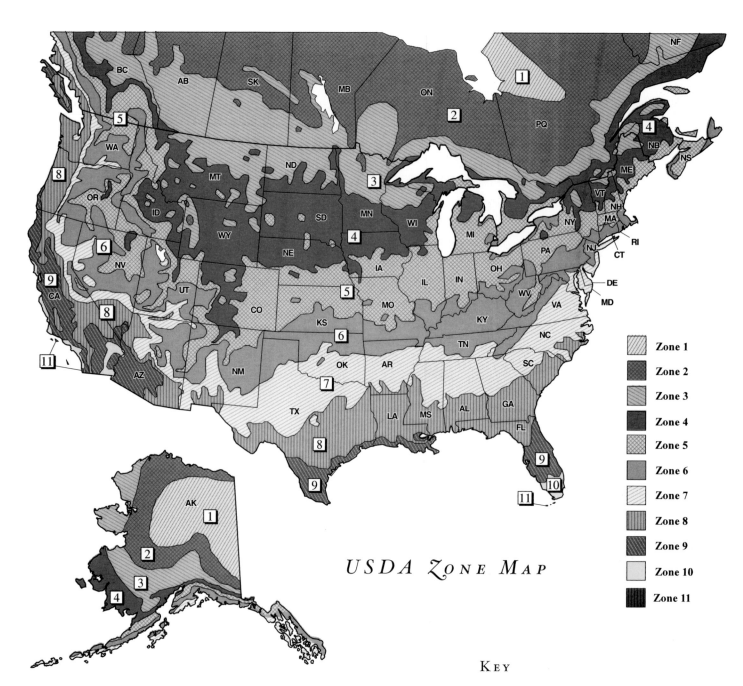

USDA Zone Map

Zone 1
Zone 2
Zone 3
Zone 4
Zone 5
Zone 6
Zone 7
Zone 8
Zone 9
Zone 10
Zone 11

KEY

ZONE	AVERAGE MIN. TEMP.	TREE PLANTING TIME
2	-50 to -40°	June 1 to September 1
3	-40 to -30°	May 15 to September 1
4	-30 to -20°	May 1 to September 15
5	-20 to -10°	April 15 to September 30
6	-10 to 0°	April 1 to October 30
7	0 to 10°	March 15 to October 30
8	10 to 20°	February 1 to November 15
9	20 to 30°	Year-round
10	30 to 40°	Year-round
11	above 40°	Year-round

JEFF'S POTTING SHED

Every tree grower needs to have supplies handy to ensure healthy plants. Here's what I keep in my potting shed:

❧ For seed processing in the refrigerator: horticultural perlite

❧ For the best germination results: Scotts Potting Soil for Seed Starting

❧ For transplanting new plants to larger containers and for preparing ground for new plants: Miracle-Gro Garden Soil for Trees and Shrubs

❧ For fertilizing new plants: water-soluble plant food 15-30-15 (use half strength)

❧ For trees in the ground after the first year: Osmocote Plant Food 14-14-14

❧ For making sharp, clean cuts and pruning undesirable branches: high-quality bypass pruners. Be sure to clean your pruning shears thoroughly after each use to prevent the spread of diseases to other plants.

❧ For preparing planting areas and edging: square-blade garden spade

❧ For moisture retention and weed control: pine bark nuggets or cypress mulch

❧ For a mold and mildew fungicide spray, mix one part household bleach with ten parts water.

❧ For larger trees and the best nut production, use tree fertilizer spikes.

 ## APPENDIX B

INFORMATION ABOUT FAMOUS AND HISTORIC TREES

HISTORIC TREE SITES

Indian Marker Pecan
The tree is now dead. You can be shown its original site by contacting the Dallas Historic Tree Coalition:
660 Preston Forest Center, Suite 407
Dallas, TX
214-739-5886
www.geocities.com/-dhtc

Berkeley Plantation Sycamore
Berkeley Hundred Plantation
Virginia Route 5
Charles City, VA
804-829-6018
www.jamesriverplantations.org

George Washington Tulip Poplar
George Washington's Mount Vernon
Mount Vernon, VA
703-799-8661
www.mountvernon.org

Patrick Henry Osage Orange
Patrick Henry National Memorial
1250 Red Hill Road
Brookneal, VA
www.redhill.org

Jacksonville Treaty Live Oak
Treaty Oak Park
Main Street at Prudential Drive
Jacksonville, FL
www.coj.com

Lewis and Clark Cottonwood
Fort Mandan Historic Site
U.S. Hwy 83 and N.D. Hwy 200A
Washburn, ND
701-462-8535
www.fortmandan.com

Andrew Jackson Southern Magnolia
The Hermitage
4580 Rachel's Lane
Hermitage, TN
615-889-2941
www.thehermitage.com

Johnny Appleseed Rambo Apple
This tree is on a private family farm.
Contact the Urbana University Johnny Appleseed Museum
Urbana, OH
937-484-1301
www.urbana.edu/appleseedworkshop

Mark Twain Cave Bur Oak
Highway 79 South
Hannibal, MO
800-527-0304
www.marktwaincave.com

Walden Woods Red Maple
915 Walden Street
Concord, MA
508-369-6993
www.walden.org/project

Gettysburg Address Honey Locust
Gettysburg National Military Park
Gettysburg, PA
717-334-1124
www.nps.gov/gett

Frederick Douglass White Oak
Frederick Douglass National Historic Site
1411 West Street
Washington, D.C.
202-426-5961
www.nps.gov/frdo/freddoug

Wyatt Earp Black Walnut
There is no public access to the privately owned home.
    Please view the tree from the street.
Wyatt Earp Home
1020 East Detroit Avenue
Monmouth, IL

Amelia Earhart Sugar Maple
223 North Terrace
Atchison, KS
913-367-4217
www.ameliaearhartmuseum.org

John F. Kennedy Post Oak
Arlington National Cemetery
Arlington, VA
903-614-9042
www.arlingtoncemetery.org

Elvis Presley Pin Oak
Graceland
3734 Elvis Presley Boulevard
Memphis, TN
800-238-2010
www.elvis-presley.com

Moon Sycamore
Mississippi State University
Mississippi State, MS
601-325-2323
www.msstate.edu

*P*LEASE *R*ESPECT *A*MERICA'S *C*ULTURAL *H*ERITAGE

We have introduced you to many trees that are national landmarks and proud survivors of our collective history. If this book inspires you to visit the "parent" trees, and we hope it does, please take photographs, but let the seeds and leaves remain intact. It is against the law to remove living plants, seeds, or cuttings from historic sites. Please allow us to be your source for authentic direct offspring of these historic trees. We grow every one of the trees depicted in this book and will gladly make them available to you. Call 1-800-320-TREE (8733) or visit www.historictrees.org. Thank you!

Young trees growing in tubes at the Famous & Historic Trees nursery.

About American Forests' Famous & Historic Trees Project

Imagine an America without its national forests, without its majestic redwoods, without the surprising coolness of city forests like Central Park. Back in 1875, Chicago physician John Aston Warder and other conservation-minded citizens became alarmed at the rampant waste of and disregard for trees. They formed the American Forestry Association and began planting and championing trees.

Now, more than 125 years later, American Forests is still planting and protecting trees. Our proud heritage includes helping create the National Forest and National Park systems; starting and maintaining the National Register of Big Trees, a registry for the largest known examples of 826 native and naturalized species; and honoring and propagating trees of historic status in America and around the world. Together with local citizens and groups, our

Global ReLeaf program has helped restore ecosystems by planting more than 15 million trees on damaged public lands.

American Forests first began compiling a list of trees connected with historic persons, events, and places in 1917. In 1988 it joined with veteran nurseryman Jeffrey Meyer to create American Forests' Famous & Historic Trees project. Over the years the program has hand-collected seeds from notable trees and carefully grown the seedlings at its state-of-the-art nursery in Jacksonville, Florida. Our collection has included more than a thousand trees, which have been planted in backyards, on state capitol grounds, and at schools, where they help students make the link between history and the world around them. In partnership with the White House Millennium Council and the Millennium Green program coordinated by the U.S. Department of Agriculture, Millennium Groves of historic trees have been planted across the country as another way to pass on our rich history to future generations.

Do you know about a historic tree? American Forests invites your participation in the National Register of Historic Trees. To nominate a tree to the register, go to www.historictrees.org or call 1-800-320-TREE (8733) to request a nomination form.

❧ ILLUSTRATION CREDITS

Line drawings throughout are by Elayne Sears.